Newly Qualified Social Workers: A Handbook for Practice

Post-qualifying Social Work Practice – titles in the series

To order, please contact our distributor: BEBC Distribution, Albion Close, Parkstone, Poole BH12 3LL. Telephone: 0845 230 9000, email: **learningmatters@bebc.co.uk**.

You can also find more information on each of these titles and our other learning resources at **www.learningmatters.co.uk**.

Newly Qualified Social Workers: A Handbook for Practice

Edited by
STEVEN KEEN, IVAN GRAY,
JONATHAN PARKER,
DI GALPIN, KEITH BROWN

Series Editor: Keith Brown

LearningMatters

First published in 2009 by Learning Matters Ltd

British Library Cataloguing in Publication Data

A CIP record for this book is available from the British Library

ISBN: 978 1 84445 251 4

Cover and text design by Code 5 Design Associates Ltd
Project management by Swales & Willis
Typeset by Swales & Willis Ltd, Exeter, Devon
Printed and bound in Great Britain by TJ International, Padstow, Cornwall

Learning Matters Ltd
33 Southernhay East
Exeter EX1 1NX
Tel: 01392 215560
info@learningmatters.co.uk
www.learningmatters.co.uk

FSC
Mixed Sources
Product group from well-managed
forests and other controlled sources
Cert no. SGS-COC-2482
www.fsc.org
© 1996 Forest Stewardship Council

Contents

About the editors

Steven Keen brings together years of wide-ranging management, research, education, consultancy, lecturing, thesis supervision and sports coaching experience in his current role as Senior Lecturer in Research within the Centre for Social Work and Social Policy at Bournemouth University.

Ivan Gray holds academic and professional qualifications in social work and management. He has specialised in management development for the past 16 years and he has also lectured in social work. He is programme leader for the BA and MA in Leadership and Management at Bournemouth University.

Jonathan Parker is currently Professor of Social Work, Director of the Centre for Social Work and Social Policy and Associate Dean at Bournemouth University. He has taught social work theory and practice for many years and has worked as a social worker and psychotherapist before starting his academic career. He is author of numerous books and articles on social work practice.

Di Galpin is a qualified social worker, having worked for 14 years in mental health, disability and older people services. She is currently a Senior Lecturer in Post-Qualifying Social Work at Bournemouth University and programme leader for the specialist award in Working with Vulnerable Adults.

Keith Brown holds academic and professional qualifications in social work, nursing, teaching and management. He has worked in the education and training field for over 20 years, in both universities and local authorities, and is currently Director of the Centre for Post-Qualifying Social Work at Bournemouth University.

Book contributors

Angela, service user Angela has personal experience of mental health services and has worked as a service user representative for the last 12 years. She has delivered training both locally and nationally and is an 'activist' for Rethink. She is a member of the Bournemouth University Carer and Service User Partnership Group and feels that her lived experience of mental illness and training experience can offer a unique perspective to newly qualified social workers.

Shelley Baker, newly qualified social worker Shelley qualified as a social worker in 2008. She completed her degree at Bournemouth University. Since qualifying she has been working as an Education Social Worker in a local authority in the South. Shelley's primary role is to work with children, young people, their families, schools and other professionals to improve school attendance and address presenting welfare issues.

Jenny Bigmore, Lecturer, Bournemouth University Jenny is a registered social worker and prior to joining Bournemouth University, worked as a social worker in both Education and Children's Services. She is now a lecturer and programme leader for the PQ Specialist Childcare Award in the Post-Qualifying Social Work Team.

Keith Brown, Director of Centre for Post-Qualifying Social Work, Bournemouth University Keith holds academic and professional qualifications in social work, nursing, teaching and management. He has worked in the education and training field for over 20 years, in universities and local authorities and is currently Director of the Centre for Post-Qualifying Social Work at Bournemouth University.

Jill Davey, Senior Lecturer, Bournemouth University Jill is a qualified social worker, with 25 years' experience of working with children and families at both a practitioner and managerial level. Jill holds academic and professional qualifications in both social work and teaching. She is currently programme leader for the BA Social Work programme and also teaches on the specialist Post-Qualifying Awards.

Marion Davis, Strategic Director of Children's Services, Warwickshire County Council Marion is Strategic Director of Children's Services for Warwickshire, with the job title of Strategic Director of Children, Young People and Families. She is a qualified social worker with nearly 30 years experience as a social worker, manager and Head of Service in both children's and adult services. She has previously worked for Dorset County Council, Devon County Council and Plymouth City Council.

Dr Lee-Ann Fenge, Senior Academic, Bournemouth University Prior to joining Bournemouth University as a lecturer in 1995, she worked as a social worker in a number of adult social services settings in London and Dorset. Her particular interests are in practice with older people and community care. She has undertaken a number of participatory action research projects with older people, and has published recent academic papers on participatory action research methodology, involving older service users in research, migrant workers in the NHS, and sexuality and bereavement. She has recently been awarded her doctorate for a study on widening participation in higher education.

Melanie Forsyth-Smith, Bournemouth University Melanie qualified in social work over 20 years ago and has held posts in fieldwork and residential care, before moving into the training and education field, working as a trainer, assessor and practice teacher in statutory, voluntary and education settings. She joined Bournemouth University when post-qualifying training was in its infancy and now is PQSW Lecturer and programme leader for the Consolidation programme. She has seen over 1700 students through the consolidation process and has marked over 400 portfolios.

Di Galpin, Senior Lecturer, Bournemouth University Di is a qualified social worker, having worked for 14 years in mental health, disability and older peoples services. She is currently a Senior Lecturer in Post-Qualifying Social Work at Bournemouth University and programme leader for the specialist award in Working with Vulnerable Adults.

George, carer George is a carer of his wife who has a personality disorder. He has cared for her for more than 17 years. They have four children aged 18,16,14 and 12 and have linked up with general practitioners, community mental health teams, social workers as well as the police in the continuing treatment of his wife. These experiences are something that he wishes to share with newly qualified social workers.

Dr Ivan Gray, Senior Lecturer, Bournemouth University Ivan holds academic and professional qualifications in social work and management. He has specialised in management development for the past 16 years, although he has also lectured in social work. He is programme leader for the BA and MA in Leadership and Management at Bournemouth University.

Mike Henry, Learning and Development Manager and Workforce Strategy Lead, Children's Services, Dorset County Council Mike is a qualified social worker and has worked in a range of practice and managerial roles in children's social care. He manages the social work education function for adults and children's directorates in Dorset and has conducted research into newly qualified social workers in children's services with Kay Renshaw.

Angela Hickin, Service Manager, children with additional needs Angela has been working in social care for 15 years and has worked within adult services, child protection, safeguarding and with community projects. Her current role is as a service manager within a combined education and social care service providing services to children with disabilities and/or special educational needs (SEN) as well as portage and early support services to children under five. Her areas of interest include improving practitioners' awareness of safeguarding issues especially in relation to children with SEN and/or disabilities;

improving outcomes for children with disabilities/SEN and encouraging joined up working between different organisations.

Kate Howe, Senior Lecturer in Social Work, Bournemouth University Kate has worked in social work/social care education for 13 years, having previously worked as a social worker in statutory and third sector agencies. At Bournemouth University she works in the undergraduate team and specialises in Practice Learning and Communication Skills.

Mark Hutton, Hospital Social Work Manager, Milton Keynes Mark qualified as a Social Worker in 1991. He currently provides leadership and management to a social work service in an acute hospital. In November 2007 he was awarded a BA Hons in Leadership and Management in Health and Social Care and a full (PQ 2-6) Post-Qualifying Social Work Award.

Dr Graham Ixer, Head of Social Work Education, General Social Care Council Graham was a social worker, manager and educator. After many years teaching and managing a social work programme he moved into policy where he led the development of the first ever codes of practice for the General Social Care Council. He is currently Head of Social Work Education at the GSCC. He is an active teacher in social policy and researcher in reflective practice and has worked in a number of universities in the UK, Sweden, USA and Japan. He has published widely including his latest book on international examples of practice learning.

Brian Jones, Health, Social Care and Wellbeing Strategy Manager, Newport Brian qualified as a social worker in 1978 working as, firstly, a generic social worker and, later, as a specialist in work with older people. Management responsibilities struck in the early 1990s and have been retained. Brian has taught with the Open University for 15 years, currently on Managing in Health and Social Care.

Dr Steven Keen, Senior Lecturer, Bournemouth University Steven brings together years of wide-ranging management, research, education, consultancy, lecturing, thesis supervision and sports coaching experience in his current role as a Senior Lecturer in Research within the Centre for Social Work and Social Policy at Bournemouth University.

Penny Lodwick, Service Manager, Dorset Penny began her social work career in London in 1980. She worked for 17 years in Southwark, initially in generic and then Child and Family Services, latterly as a Senior Practitioner before moving to Dorset to take up the Team Manager post at Christchurch in Dorset. She held this position for 10 years including working as a Locality Co-ordinatior on secondment. She was appointed Service Manager in 2008.

Marion Macdonald, Workforce Strategy Staff Development and Training Manager Marion Macdonald is a Social Care Workforce Strategy Manager. She has 12 years experience in statutory social care training teams, both as a trainer and a training manager. Marion worked directly with people with Learning Difficulties for 9 years before and after qualifying as a social worker in 1992.

Anne Quinney, Senior Lecturer, Bournemouth University Anne is a Senior Lecturer in Social Work at Bournemouth University. She is the author of *Collaborative Social Work Practice* and Editor of the journal *Practice: Social Work in Action*, a journal of the British

Association of Social Workers (BASW). Anne is a qualified social worker and has worked as a social worker and youth worker in Dorset and in Scotland.

Professor Jonathan Parker, Associate Dean and Director of the Centre for Social Work and Social Policy, Bournemouth University Jonathan has taught social work theory and practice for many years, and has worked as a social worker and psychotherapist before starting his academic career. He is author of numerous books and articles on social work practice.

Patricia, carer Patricia is the carer of a young man with Down's Syndrome who was her foster child from the age of two weeks. Life experiences and work with around 20 social workers in the last 27 years has given her things to share which she hopes are of value to newly qualified social workers.

Emma Perry, social worker Emma completed her Masters Degree and Diploma in Social Work at Keele University in 2004. Since then she has worked for a Midlands-based council on an Older Persons Team. She has undertaken a variety of roles on the team and is currently a GP Linked Practitioner.

Kay Renshaw, Senior Learning and Development Officer, Dorset County Council Kay Renshaw is a qualified social worker and has worked primarily in child protection; she also holds the Practice Teacher Award. Kay now works in a Learning and Development Team as Senior Learning and Development Officer responsible for the co-ordination and support of social work students and practice teachers, developing the NQSW pilot as well as co-ordinating and supporting post-qualifying awards. Kay, along with Mike Henry, undertook research on the experiences of NQSW's to inform her practice and work with newly qualified social workers.

Lynne Rutter, Lecturer, Bournemouth University Lynne Rutter is a lecturer on Post-Qualifying Social Work Award units 'Enabling Work-Based Learning' (H level) and 'Leading and Enabling Others' (M level). She also provides academic support to all students undertaking PQSW programmes. She has developed a keen interest in all aspects of professional education, in particular experiential and reflective learning for professional practitioners who are undertaking HE programmes. In 2005, she was awarded a Bournemouth University Learning and Teaching Fellowship.

Clare Seymour, Senior Lecturer in Social Work Clare is a Senior Lecturer and Admissions Tutor in Social Work at Anglia Ruskin University. She is involved in teaching social work law, communication and interviewing skills, and professional accountability to social work students at undergraduate and masters level. Her social work experience includes 16 years of local authority social work, latterly in a childcare team where she had wide experience of court work, and bereavement support within a general practice. One of her most recent texts *Courtroom Skills for Social Workers* (2007) has been co-authored with a Senior Circuit Judge who is assigned to the Queen's Bench Division of the High Court and is also published by Learning Matters.

Martha Sharp, newly qualified social worker Martha Sharp began her training at the age of 20, completing a three year degree in social work at Bournemouth University; here she accomplished two 100-day placements, both in Adult and Children's Services. Shortly after graduating from her training in 2008, she found employment in a local authority childcare assessment team, where she has started her career as a newly qualified social worker.

Liz Slinn, newly qualified social worker Liz works for a County Council in the South of England, in a locality team working with children and families, including Children in Need, Child Protection and Looked After Children. She completed her social work degree at the University of Reading following the employment route training. Liz previously worked as a family support worker, a classroom assistant with children with emotional and behavioural problems, and cared for a boy with autism as part of a year out with Community Service Volunteers.

Richard Williams, Senior Lecturer, Bournemouth University Richard is a qualified social worker with 34 years' experience of working with children and families at both practitioner and managerial level. He is currently a senior lecturer in Social Work for the BA Social Work programme.

Anna Woodruff, newly qualified social worker Anna is a social worker for an adult care team in the South West of England. She was part of the first intake for the new social work degree, studying at Trowbridge College. She has been in practice for over two years now and is keen to see what her future in social work holds.

Foreword

Professor David Croisdale-Appleby
Chair, Skills for Care

As the Sector Skills Council with direct responsibility for developing the skills and knowledge of the adult social care workforce we know just how important it is to make every one of the 1.5 million people who work in the sector get good quality support, supervision and development opportunities throughout their careers.

But this is especially true for Newly Qualified Social Workers (NQSWs). As employers and new social workers tell us, the first year of practice is absolutely vital as they bridge the gap between what they've learnt during their degree and their new frontline duties.

As we developed our framework for NQSWs we identified a number of factors that impact on whether social workers stay in the profession including:

- NQSWs need support to build on the expertise and knowledge they have developed on qualifying programmes and how to apply this to a practice setting as qualified workers.

- Good quality induction to the profession and to their organisation.

- Access to the correct type and quality of supervision.

- A structured process of continued professional development supporting them to develop their career beyond first year practice.

In an age where the social work profession often feels under threat and undervalued, we recognise that leadership and management is vital in making sure the day to day work of most social workers continues to be of an incredibly high standard. That's why we have created a Leadership and Management strategy and a Leadership and Management qualification for aspiring managers.

A vital role for those leaders and managers is making sure NQSWs get the high quality supervision and support they need in the early days of their careers. On a practical level we have produced a very popular Supervision Unit that helps managers supervise their staff in a straightforward and consistent way, and have built on this with supervision guidance for NQSWs.

At a strategic level, we have joined forces with the Department of Health to distribute £4 million in funding to support individual students and supervisors. Students and supervisors get £1000 each to create the time and space necessary to have considered supervision. This grant has proved very popular with 100% take up of the available funds.

Our innovative work on how Post-Qualifying (PQ) projects can be used to support the needs of NQSWs is rightly cited in this publication as highlighting the real need for social workers to access PQ qualifications to ensure they develop sustainable long-term careers.

Skills for Care believes this publication brings together some of the best current thinking about how we can support NQSWs, but also offers practical solutions to how we can offer real practical support to new graduates coming into the social work profession.

New ways of supporting and developing NQSWs has never been more important as they will play a vital part in restoring public confidence in the profession.

Preface

There has probably never been a time such as now when the social work profession is under the spotlight. It feels like hardly a week passes by without some aspect of social work being in the national press.

Against this ever changing background and questioning of the role and nature of social work, there has been a genuine desire from the Department of Health (DH) and the Department for Children, Schools and Families (DCSF) to support newly qualified social workers as they bridge the gap from student to qualified social work professional. To support this transition the DCSF launched their strategy for newly qualified childcare social workers in 2008, shortly followed in March 2009 with the DH's strategy to support newly qualified social workers working with adults.

To dovetail with this emphasis of providing better support to newly qualified social workers we decided, here at the Centre for Post-Qualifying Social Work at Bournemouth University, to write a comprehensive handbook designed to help newly qualified workers as they launch their careers. To this end, and with the notable help of managers from practice, newly qualified social workers, carers, people who use services and colleagues, we have produced this handbook.

We hope that the various and wide-ranging contributions and insight will indeed help you, the newly qualified social worker, to bridge the gap between student and professional. As such, this handbook is full of practical tasks, advice and guidance. It is our sincere desire that it helps to develop the social work profession to reach even higher standards of professional activity. This handbook has also been designed to help you embark on a journey of continuous professional development and points to the Post-Qualifying Social Work framework as one of the vehicles to achieve this.

All the Learning Matters texts in the Post-Qualifying Social Work Practice series have been written by people with a passion for excellence in social work practice. This handbook is no different. The other books in this series may also be of value to you, as a newly qualified social worker, as they are written to inform, inspire and develop social work practice.

To all newly qualified social workers, we wish you well in your professional career.

Keith Brown
Series Editor
Director, Centre for Post-Qualifying Social Work, Bournemouth University

Acknowledgements

This has been an unusual book to write and indeed edit. On the back of wanting to make more of a difference with our newly qualified social worker research in the South West region, Ivan Gray first had the idea of producing this handbook. Fifteen months later we (the editors) are so very grateful to over 30 contributors – a wonderful mix of people who use services, carers, service, strategy and learning and development managers, experienced and newly qualified social workers alike, employers, contributors from regulatory bodies and academics – heart-felt thanks to you all. Thank you also to all the anonymous peer reviewers from the above mentioned groups. And finally, thank you to Luke Block and Lauren Simpson for keeping us all, very cheerfully, on track.

Chapter 1
Please mind the gap

Steven Keen and Jonathan Parker

How many times have you heard the familiar words 'mind the gap'? In the late 1960s it became impractical for London Underground staff continually to warn passengers about the gap between train and platform. The equivalent phrase in France, Hong Kong, Singapore, Australia and the United States highlights the same problem – trains do not quite fit their stations. Likewise, newly qualified social workers often find they do not fit comfortably into their new organisations. Whether you have qualified as a social worker in England (Brown *et al.*, 2007), Ireland (National Social Work Qualifications Board (NSWQB), 2004) or Australia (McDonald, 2007) appears to make no difference – the breach between qualification and first post is likely to be significant. Newly qualified social workers (NQSW) describe their first year in practice using very graphic terms.

- *It was a baptism of fire* (Bates *et al.*, 2009, p 21).

- *I constantly felt I was just keeping my head above water* (Revans, 2008, p 15).

Whether you are a newly qualified social worker or someone who is about to qualify, this book will help you to mind that gap.

Most social work textbooks focus on social work practice, social work skills or on how to study for your social work degree. None of these texts directly address the gap or crucial transition period between finishing off the social work degree and managing the first years of practice. As such, this book offers down to earth, practical guidance on applying for your first post and managing your first few years. It includes useful sections on topics such as induction, supervision, dealing with conflict, post-qualifying awards, court skills, report writing, and team working – and is written by a group of over 30 authors with extensive qualifying and post-qualifying social work education, and social work practice experience – be they people who use services, carers, managers, academics, or newly qualified social workers.

Our interest in this transition period was fired by a recent research project tracking the learning and development needs of 22 newly qualified social workers in the south-west (UK) region (Brown *et al.*, 2007). It is to this research project, we turn briefly.

The first social workers to graduate with the new degree did so in the summer of 2006. Later that year, Skills for Care commissioned Bournemouth University to track newly qualified social workers in the South West region through their first year of employment. They asked us to do three things:

- to evaluate their perceptions of the effectiveness of the new social work degree;
- to evaluate their perceptions of the effectiveness of their induction and/or probation periods;
- to track their progress towards post-qualifying social work education.

We also sought the perspective of people who use services, carers, and line managers on the learning and development needs of these newly qualified social workers. What we found out through the use of multiple questionnaires, interviews, and focus groups surprised us.

Blewitt and Tunstall (2008) raise the question whether generic qualifying programmes enable social workers to work equally well in children's *and* adult services. Recent unpublished research suggests the answer is 'no'; just one-third of newly qualified children's workers believe their degree course prepared them for their jobs (Sellick, 2008). However, in our sample (all from local authority children's or adult services) about three-quarters of newly qualified social workers and their line managers agreed that the social work degree provided workers with the right knowledge, understanding, and skills for their current post – a finding that remained almost constant over the nine months of the evaluation (Bates *et al.*, 2009). The recent evaluation of England's social work degree reports a similarly positive experience of teaching and learning (Evaluation of Social Work Degree Qualifications in England Team (ESWDQET), 2008). Yet, this study and Brown *et al.* (2007) report negative findings. About a quarter of our sample did not feel prepared by their qualifying programme in areas such as assessment, report writing, dealing with conflict, and care management; the issue that stood out though was the development of court skills (Brown *et al.*, 2007; Bates *et al.*, 2009).

About three-quarters of our sample underwent a workplace-based induction. Yet, during interviews it became clear that few had been given a structured induction – that is, one that helped them move into their new role in a clear, planned and organised fashion. As far as the probation period is concerned, just over half the newly qualified social workers found this period useful. Finally, three newly qualified social workers claimed to know nothing about post-qualifying social work education – this, of course, was *not* confirmed by their line managers.

You will notice from the contents page that this handbook is a result of and a response to these research findings, and we have used your colleagues' experiences to structure it. These findings have even fuelled debates in the House of Lords (Hansard, 2007) on the need for newly qualified social workers to have a 'protected year', like newly qualified teachers, in which they consolidate their learning and development as they start to practise (Sale, 2007). Subsequent to these debates, the government asked the Children's Workforce Development Council (CWDC) to develop a three-year pilot programme (£27m) for newly qualified social workers working in children's services to help them strengthen their knowledge, skills and confidence (DfES/DH, 2006; CWDC, 2008, 2008a). This programme started in September 2008 and has an annual intake of about 1,000 newly qualified social workers. CWDC highlights 11 outcome statements that a newly qualified social worker needs to know, understand, and be able to do by the end of their first year in practice (CWDC, 2008, 2008a). Each newly qualified childcare worker is provided with a structured induction to help consolidate previous learning, protected time (10 per cent) for development and training activity, and structured and regular supervision. Skills for Care (2008) have recently followed suit and published draft details on their newly qualified adult social worker framework and 12 outcome statements. Both programmes intend a smooth transition from qualifying training to practice and will be successful if they are fully supported by employers with a commitment to provide high quality supervision, mentoring and support from experienced and qualified social workers.

These welcome interventions come at a time of continued change in the world of social work practice resulting from radical reform of the public sector (Jordan and Jordan, 2006). Since the New Labour government was first elected in 1997, the social and health care sector has been subject to a 'modernising' agenda heralded by the Department of Health (DH) White Paper *Modernising Social Services* (DH, 1998). This agenda focuses on public service improvement through increased regulation, inspection, and monitoring (Parker, 2007). Alongside this, services have been rationalised, some prioritised, and some integrated with others. Children and families' services have, in many authorities, been separated from adult social care. There is an increasing emphasis on working collaboratively with other disciplines and agencies to improve services rather than being constrained by their professional roles (Barr *et al.*, 2008; Quinney, 2006). The involvement of carers and people who use services in designing and leading services has been promoted (Beresford, 2003; DH, 2007, 2008). The Care Standards Act 2000 and our professional regulator's code of practice (General Social Care Council (GSCC), 2004) require commitment and adherence. Employing agencies will require social workers to contribute to performance assessment frameworks and service inspections to promote improvement and development (Sinclair, 2008). Treading a path through such a complex world requires models of social work practice that maintain the value base, yet can also facilitate the development of services and their management and promote personal and professional growth.

This handbook should help you tread such a path. The flow of the chapters that follow is logical in that Chapter 2 starts with the transition period between finishing off the social work degree and starting a new job. This chapter will assist you to think through issues not only around choosing your first social work post but also tips on how to apply for it. Chapter 3 will help you to clarify your expectations regarding induction, probation and supervision – and sketches out your role and responsibilities within these processes Chapter 4 summarises good practice and professional requirements in relation to Continuing Professional Development (CPD) and Post-Registration Training and Learning (PRTL) – these form the foundation to an outline of post-qualifying award opportunities and how best to prepare for them during your first years of practice.

Chapter 5 addresses specific personal issues such as self-awareness, stress, and the management of conflict whilst the final two chapters focus on the workplace. Chapter 6 reiterates to the reader the team, partnership and multidisciplinary nature of social work practice working – while Chapter 7 will help you understand your potential contribution to the development of services within the context of business planning, managerialism, and learning organisations. The remaining appendices pick up on those findings we mentioned earlier that are not covered in the above chapters – they are designed to be helpful snapshots for newly qualified social workers into issues such as assessment, care management and contracting, court skills, writing skills, post-qualifying awards and child protection; providing signposts along the way. Further reading sections, practical tasks, critical commentaries, and case studies within both appendices and chapters, written by managers, people who use services, carers, experienced practitioners, newly qualified social workers and academics bring alive the above topics – and make this book what it is intended to be – a practical, down to earth handbook for newly qualified (or about to qualify) social workers entering their first years of practice.

NB Please note that many of the real names of newly qualified social workers, carers and people who use services have been given pseudonyms.

FURTHER READING

The Children's Workforce Development Council have a designated website section for newly qualified social workers and their pilot programme. Available from: **www.cwdcouncil.org.uk/nqsw** (accessed 16 February 2009).

Skills for Care have also given over part of their website to the development of newly qualified social workers. Available from: **www.skillsforcare.org.uk/developing_skills/social_work/Newly QualifiedSocialWorkers.aspx?** (accessed 16 February 2009).

Chapter 2

Managing transitions

Lee Ann Fenge with contributions from Mark Hutton (manager), Tom (NQSW) and Tom's university tutors

This chapter will help you to prepare for the following National Occupational Standards for Social Work.

● Key role 1, unit 1: Prepare for social work contact and involvement.

● Key role 5: Manage and be accountable for your own social work practice.

Introduction

In this chapter you will consider the impact that acquiring a new role as a qualified social worker has on you, and ways of planning for such a change of status. This process will involve developing self-awareness and adaptability in the face of change. There should be resonance here with the knowledge and experience you will have gained as a social work student in terms of working with individuals who face change and transitions within their life course. The knowledge and experience you will have gained as part of your social work degree therefore has application to the transitions and changes you will encounter in the early stages of your practice as a social worker. This chapter is structured to help you to prepare for the transition from student to qualified social work practitioner so that your transition is successful, with the minimum of stress and disruption.

You will have been working towards this point throughout your qualifying education. Indeed, your journey to a career within social work may have been much longer, including achieving relevant work experience and qualifications to gain entry onto a social work degree. This can be viewed as a voluntary transition, where you have had time to consider the various options open to you (Fouad and Bynner, 2008).

You may have been clear at the start of your degree about the area in which you ultimately want to practise, or this may have gradually emerged during the course of your studies and experience on placement. You may be surprised that the area you are now considering for a career, or are engaged in as a qualified practitioner, is not something you would have considered at the start of your degree. You may still be unclear as to what type of setting and user group you eventually want to work with, and may still be considering several options. This is a time of opportunity and change, and it is important that you reflect deeply on where you want your career to develop and what opportunities might be open to you. Chapter 4 should be further help to you here as it addresses your continuing professional development.

As a newly qualified practitioner, the first few weeks and months of your life in the professional community *can set the stage for a successful and gratifying career – or lead to stagnation, disillusionment and attrition* (Pare and Le Maistre, 2006, p 363). It is therefore important that you anticipate and prepare well for this transition from student to qualified social work practitioner. No doubt you will also face continued transitions throughout your professional life as you choose to specialise in particular areas of practice.

Transition research

So, what does research tell us about the transition from student to practitioner? Research into trends of social work employment suggests graduates enter employment quickly, with over half in 1996 and 2001 working in social work within one month of graduating (Lyons and Manion, 2004). In a survey of newly qualified social workers' experiences although 75 per cent described themselves as ready for practice, 50 per cent believed that their work was different from their previous expectations (Marsh and Triseliotis, 1996). More recently, Plymouth and Durham universities have attempted to identify what works in terms of the transition from student to competent social work practitioner (Revans, 2008). They found that most newly qualified social workers struggle with the duality of their roles and need support in establishing coping mechanisms and work life balance (Revans, 2008).

We can also draw on research from the nursing and the allied health professions to help understand the impact of transition from student to qualified practitioner. It is suggested that newly qualified nursing graduates often experience feelings of being unprepared – which can lead to stress when entering the workforce for the first time (Newton and McKenna, 2006; Gerrish, 2000). Other research suggests that the experience of being a newly qualified nurse can lead to feelings of uncertainty and chaos (Wangensteen *et al.*, 2008). Similarly, newly qualified doctors highlight that increased responsibility can lead to strong feelings of uncertainty (Prince *et al.*, 2004). Concerns about increased accountability and responsibility and feelings of being *in over one's head* are also reported in research with newly qualified youth care professionals (Moscrip and Brown, 2002). Mismatches between the expectations of newly qualified speech therapists, their employers and universities are also reported in the literature (Brumfitt *et al.*, 2005).

What can we conclude from this research? Simply this – the transition from student to newly qualified practitioner, across a range of disciplines can be stressful and unsettling. It involves a process of moving from the culture of an educational establishment to the organisational culture of the workplace (Schrader, 2008); a process of seeing oneself as a graduate practitioner; a process of developing an awareness of your own expectations and what they mean; and a process of understanding the expectations of your new employer and colleagues as well. Although you will have gained practice experience through social work placements, the status of a student social worker in placement is different from that of a newly qualified social worker. The expectations you have of your own practice, the expectations of your employer, and the expectations of people who use services and carers may be different, and part of your transition will be to cope with any mismatch that exists. This process involves you moving on from being immersed in your higher education 'community of practice' to your social work practitioner 'community of practice' (Wenger, 1998). Therefore, you are, or will be, engaged in a process of sense-making (Weick, 1995); one in which you are making sense of your changing identity from that of a student to a newly qualified practitioner.

Sense-making

Weick (1995, p 17) identifies six characteristics of sense-making. Sense-making is:

● grounded in identity production – your emerging identity as a social work practitioner;

● retrospective – we rely on what we know to make sense of our present situation;

● enactive of sensible environments – the organisational environment plays a key role in the way you make sense of yourself as a practitioner; we therefore rely on what others are doing to frame our understanding of events;

● social – we do not make sense of ourselves in a vacuum and our understanding is often contingent on the conduct of others;

● ongoing – sense-making never stops as it is an ongoing process;

● focused on and by extracted cues – we rely on cues that we extract from our working environment, and which we use to make it seem plausible: therefore sense-making processes are driven by what is plausible rather than by what is accurate.

Weick (1995, p 20) suggests that how you make sense of your situation is grounded in the identity you develop of yourself in relation to others. So, in developing your professional identity it is important that you look back to the experiences that have been influential in the past, as well as being aware of the factors that will influence you in your new post. It is also important to remind yourself of your successes and positive experiences to ensure that you carry them with you into your new job.

ACTIVITY **2.1**

Preparing for transition – assessing your own growth and achievement as a student social worker

A number of elements are involved in a successful transition from student to newly qualified social worker, which include recognising the knowledge and transferable skills you have acquired throughout the social work degree. Often it is easy to underestimate or forget all the strengths that you already have. This task requires that you review and list specific areas of growth and achievement as a student social worker. For example, this may include the experience of group work gained in placement, or a specific area you studied on your course.

What changes have taken place for you over the past three years; have there been pivotal learning experiences? What were the most important and/or pivotal learning experiences? What were the biggest challenges? What will you build on or try to replicate in your new post?

ACTIVITY **2.1** *(CONT.)*

At the end of the exercise, review the list. Is it longer than you expected? Are there any surprises included on it?

This exercise, and the activity tasks contained in Chapter 4, will not only enable you to review your own growth and development, but may help you identify areas that you need to develop further in the future. For example, you may feel your understanding and practice experience has provided you with grounding in mental health policy and practice, but that you really want to develop a better understanding of the Mental Capacity Act 2005 (DH, 2005).

Transitions and role change

A transition has been described as a *discontinuity in a person's life space* (Adams *et al.* 1976, p 5). There are many different types of transition that we encounter during our lives. However, as discussed earlier in the chapter, the transition you currently face as a soon to be, or newly qualified social worker is something that you have control over and you can plan for.

Research suggests that if we can anticipate change or choose to make a change, we are able to adjust more readily to the transition (Blair, 2000). To adapt successfully from student to qualified worker, it is important to prepare and plan for this transition – which might mean not applying for (and accepting) the first job you come across. This preparation involves taking time to plan what options are open to you, and what might be your most suitable first post to assist you in your longer term career goals. Research exploring factors influencing career choice highlights the importance of professional socialisation (Rubin *et al.*, 1986). Your academic study *and* placement experiences will have influenced your choice of career focus – together with other factors such as your individual characteristics, friends and family.

Even though the transition from student to qualified practitioner is planned in some way, each individual will perceive the change differently, and will cope with the transition in a different way (Parkes, 1971). Personal choice and decision making are important for both perceptions and outcomes of transitions (Ronka *et al.*, 2003). So, how will you as an individual take control of and adjust to the change from student to qualified practitioner? Blair (2000) offers a helpful four stage model of work role transition – consisting of cycles of preparation, encounters, adjustment, and stabilisation – we explore each one in turn before considering how you might find a job.

Preparation

Think about the changes you will face in your transition from student to qualified social worker. These might be positive such as changes in your financial status from student to paid qualified worker, or negative in terms of losing the support of your student peer group. The following list offers suggestions but is not exhaustive.

- *Identity* – at the crux of any transition from student to qualified worker is a change in identity. This not only means that other people will see you differently, but you will also think about yourself differently, once qualified. You may feel relieved that your years of study are over for the time being, but you may also sense fear and a little trepidation. Koerin *et al.* (1990) suggest that as the transition from student to qualified social worker involves endings, students may react in many different ways. This may mean that *some students become overwhelmed by the thought of being in the real world* (Koerin *et al.*, 1990, p 202) and as a result try to avoid these thoughts by delaying looking for a social work job. Others may become overly anxious and invest inordinate time and energy in the job search process. It is therefore important to recognise how being qualified makes you feel, and think about how you can manage these feelings by taking control of, and making decisions about, your future.

- *Relationships* – how will the end of your life as a student social worker impact on your relationships? For the past three years you have been part of a student cohort, and may have experienced both positive and negative experiences with your peer group. Inevitably, the end of your studies will mean moving on from your current peer group and the support you may have derived from them. Try to anticipate any feelings of loss that may be associated with this process, and explore ways of coping with this change.

- *Living arrangements* – where will you live after the end of your studies? Does the end of your student life also mean a change in your living arrangements? For example, have you been sharing a house with fellow students?

- *Location* – will you remain in the same location as your university, return to your family home and/or relocate to find work? What impact might any of these decisions have on your existing support networks?

Encounter

Once you have been appointed to your first newly qualified role, it will be useful to explore what your expectations of this role are. The reality of the workplace could be very different from your expectations (Marsh and Triseliotis, 1996). Try writing down any expectations you have – about the induction period, the type of work you will be undertaking, quality of supervision, support of colleagues and the nature of the workplace you are about to enter. It may be useful to review this list two or three months into your new working life when you have encountered the realities of practice as a newly qualified practitioner. At that time, ask yourself if there is a mismatch between your expectations and the reality of practice? If there is, it might be worth asking yourself the question, what can I do about this? What can you live with and what can you change or adjust to? Chapter 5 will be further help to you in this area.

Adjustment

Adjusting successfully to a newly qualified practitioner role is essential for future confidence as a practitioner, and is a critical factor if a worker is to continue to practise in that field (Moscrip and Brown, 2002). Adjusting successfully to the transition from student to qualified practitioner involves personal change, role development and relationship building. Essential to this process is the gaining of support from your supervisor and the wider team, and managing your induction. These themes, in particular, are discussed in more detail in the next chapter and Chapter 6 (joining and contributing to a team).

Stabilisation

Successful adjustment will lead to stabilisation in your new role. This will involve increased trust, commitment, and effectiveness involving both the tasks you undertake and the people you work with. A key part of achieving a feeling of stability in your work role is increasing your competence as a practitioner. Support from colleagues and managers is also vital in building confidence during this time (Brumfitt *et al.*, 2005). The following sub-section considers how you might find a job.

Finding a job

The vacancy situation can vary across the country, thereby affecting the availability of posts. It may not be possible to get an ideal fit between the type of post you want, in the exact setting and location you desire. You may need to be flexible in your expectations, and take a view that your first role is a *stepping stone* to open up new experiences and broaden future horizons. It will be important to reflect upon your own expectations for your first qualified post.

Social workers can do many different types of jobs in a wide variety of settings, including the statutory, voluntary, and private sectors; although most newly qualified social workers appear to choose the statutory sector for their first post (Bates *et al.*, 2009). Making a decision about where you want to work in your first post is crucial and will set you on your path to future career development. A key element of the rite of *passage* from student to qualified practitioner is your registration with the General Social Care Council (GSCC). You can apply online for registration on the GSCC website (**www.gscc.org.uk**).

Career choice and targeting your career search

There are many different ways to begin your search for a social work job. You may be considering posts within the statutory, voluntary, and/or private sectors so it is important to cast your net widely when looking for adverts. Think about using the following five ideas.

- Use social networks to identify employment opportunities: through your placement experiences you may have already established some social networks to alert you to jobs that are coming up. It is therefore a good idea to keep in contact with former colleagues that you have worked alongside during your placements.

- The world wide web: the internet makes it easy to search websites such as **www. communitycare.co.uk/jobs** and **www.baswjobs.com** for social work vacancies. Many local authorities and recruitment agencies also have their own websites, so that a search for suitable jobs can be at your finger tips.

- Newspapers: newspapers such as *The Guardian* often advertise social work posts on a weekly basis, together with the local press.

- Open days or job fairs: some employers will hold open days or job fairs.

- Recruitment agencies: if appropriate, think about using national and/or local social work/care recruitment agencies.

Applying for a new social work role

Here are some suggestions which may increase your chances of being called for interview.

- Presenting yourself effectively to a prospective employer is very important and should not be underestimated, as this is the first stage in the selection process. Many agencies have a 'safe recruitment' process which means that your application may be rejected if you do not provide a full employment history with all dates accounted for. Other applications may be eliminated straight away if they are poorly presented or generally appear vague.

- A well-prepared job application is essential, as it represents all a prospective employer will know about you until the interview stage. You may be required to complete a specific application form, and/or provide an up to date Curriculum Vitae (CV). The CV should provide enough information in a clear and concise manner, avoiding unnecessary frills. It should be written in a clear format, using not less than a 12-point font. A well-structured format will include sub-headings to help the reader identify key issues. Include your skills, competencies, qualifications, and experience, and highlight your unique selling points and strengths. You will need to persuade the prospective employer that you are the right person for the job. A muddled, complicated or overly long CV will be less attractive.

- Make sure that you follow the instructions sent to you in the information pack. If you are requested to complete a handwritten application form, make sure that your presentation is neat. As applications are often photocopied; it is important to use a good quality black pen. Also, look for key words within the job description and/or person specification, and make sure that you refer to those that apply to you. Use the job description and/or person specification to structure your application and/or your CV to show those short-listing that you have the characteristics they are looking for. Use *their* wording to help signpost *your* application.

- Make sure that your spelling and grammar are correct, and that the application reads coherently. Ask someone else to check your application before you send it off.

- Keep a copy of your application form. If you get an interview make sure you study it prior to attendance. Keeping a copy will also help you to complete other applications in the future.

- You will normally be asked to provide two referees. At least one should be able to comment on your educational background, and this may be your personal tutor or another person nominated by your university. If you have a choice, select someone who can comment on both your academic ability and practice experience. It is courteous to inform referees each time you apply for a different post, so that they do not unexpectedly receive requests.

What follows is a series of three case studies. The first is a newly qualified social worker's account on applying for his first job – the second is the university perspective on Tom's account – and the final case study is an employer's perspective (unrelated to Tom).

CASE STUDY **2.1**

Tom: applying for my first job

I made the decision in year two of the social work degree that the area of practice that I wanted to pursue as a qualified worker was education social work. Tutors were encouraging us to start applying for jobs prior to finishing the course which at the time felt like an added pressure, but I now appreciate this encouragement. It was a struggle to contemplate completing application forms and preparing for interviews whilst struggling to meet the demands of assignment deadlines. However, when I saw an advertisement for education social workers in April 2008, I knew that I should take this opportunity since these jobs were fairly rare. I would advise you to start applying early if there are jobs which you are interested in.

I was advised to contact the team manager to have an informal chat prior to applying. I was really pleased I did this because it reassured me that being a newly qualified worker wouldn't disadvantage me. It also gave me an indication of what I should be researching in preparation for the interview and enabled a degree of familiarity when I was interviewed – both put me at ease.

On receipt of the application form I experienced feelings of self-doubt when I saw the essential and desirable criteria. This was when I contacted my tutor for support. She reinforced to me that skills are transferable and enabled me to see that I actually had much of the experience that they were looking for, just in a different area of practice. Don't be put off applying for a job when you see the criteria, just draw on the skills, knowledge and expertise that you do have. My tutor also highlighted the importance of being concise, since employers don't want to read an essay about you.

In preparation for the interview, I arranged to see the tutor who specialised in this area of practice. He was able to give me guidance on what the current issues are and the key documents, legislation and so on that I should familiarise myself with. This was really beneficial since it saved me time from ploughing through the wealth of information that I had found on the internet.

The interview consisted of a written assessment followed by a verbal interview with three panel members. Time management was essential for the written assessment since it would have been easy to spend the whole time on the first question! In terms of the interview I was pleased that I'd read through my application form numerous times, as much of what they asked me was based on that. When asking people for interview tips, something that kept coming up was to make sure that I had some questions ready. Knowing that I had these under my belt gave me confidence and turned the tables, since I was effectively interviewing the job to see if it was suitable for me. I was offered one of the posts and started in June 2008.

As you can see from the case study, identifying your chosen area, and seizing opportunities when they arise are key to securing your first social work position. This includes remaining vigilant to job opportunities and adverts whilst still in your final year, and drawing on the expertise of university tutors through the application process. Preparing for your interview includes finding out as much as you can about the setting and context of practice, including relevant policies and legislation. These points are reinforced by Tom's university tutors.

CASE STUDY **2.2**

Asking for help: the university perspective

How do you go from being a supported student, surrounded by people who care about your learning and development who have often vast amounts of knowledge and contacts in the social care field, to being a newly qualified social worker in full time social work practice?

When Tom obtained an interview to work as an education social worker he spoke to his tutor to ask for advice about the interview. His tutor passed Tom along to me as I had up to date experience of working in the educational field and a feel for the issues that the manager who was leading the service would be facing. This manager would most likely be assessing the interviewee as someone who could contribute to these current issues. Tom and I sat down for two hours, with an open e-mail to be used to attach files that we were talking about, for example, current Department for Schools, Children and Families guidance, up-to-date evaluations of Children Trusts and what works to improve school attendance, including documentation surrounding persistent absences.

I knew that Tom was a hard worker, so I knew he would do his research. Tom was happy to do the reading and had the interpersonal skills to communicate effectively at interview. I knew the Head of Service, who was likely to be leading the interview, would be keenly focused on the need to respond to schools identified as having persistent absence. So, when Tom went into the interview he was up to date with current issues, demonstrated he had done some research, linked current issues with evidence of what has a positive impact and had the inter-personal skills to communicate this effectively. Tom was appointed and, naturally, was delighted. He got the job in preference to other candidates who had more experience and were potentially better qualified. The feedback that Tom received was that he impressed by being well prepared; he had researched the role effectively and was clearly enthusiastic. It's really important that you talk to people who know the field.

As the tutors indicate, while they can provide guidance this is no substitute for being well prepared in order to impress a prospective employer. This is why an employer's or manager's perspective is so helpful at this point in the chapter.

CASE STUDY *2.3*

Mark Hutton: the employer perspective

Applying for your first social work post will be a new experience for you – you are likely to be overwhelmed with the application process and all it seems to entail. Think about how you can convey a sense of your commitment, experience and interest in the post you are applying for, highlighting your strengths, what attributes you can bring to the post and what your learning needs are likely to be. I am more likely to be interested in your application if you can give a concise account of yourself and what you feel would be your contribution to the job you are applying for, as well as being able to clearly identify your likely development and learning needs.

Remember that your application is likely to be one of the many that I receive and it is important that you convey a real sense of yourself (your skills, knowledge and experience) within it, as this will bring it to life, making it more interesting for the short listing panel to read, but remember, 'be concise'!

If you are unsure as to whether to apply for a post in the first instance, and if informal enquiries are welcomed as part of the application process, consider the questions you want to ask, and make contact with the employer. I'm sure they will be very willing to answer any questions you may have, and this process should portray to you a sense of the job, which you will be able to transfer into your application and use later in preparation for interview.

When completing the application form, look at the essential and desirable criteria outlined in the job description and person specification and ensure you demonstrate your skills, knowledge and experience by making reference to them using work, placement and personal experiences. If there is an area of the essential criteria where you have limited skills, do not let this put you off continuing with the application. Instead, identify what you believe you would need to do to 'fill the gap', then set to gathering the evidence through research, making reference to your findings in the application form, and how you would expect to develop your experience if you were the successful candidate. Most employers, when taking on a newly qualified social worker, will be just as keen to understand the motivation, interest and enthusiasm of the person applying for the job, alongside their skills and experience of the tasks required to fulfil the job requirements.

If you are short listed for interview you will have already conveyed a good account of yourself. The interview is your opportunity to meet us, the employer, and is as much for you to decide if you like what you see, as it is for the employer to find out about you. Interviews can be in differing formats, but the questions covered will certainly relate to the job purpose, essential and desirable criteria, the person specification, and current practice, so be prepared! If you don't understand the question, ask for it to be clarified, and take your time giving a response. Make reference to the statements you made in the application form where they are relevant to the question being answered, expanding on them where you feel confident to do so. Finally, where the employer asks you if you have any specific questions to ask them, a well prepared candidate will ask questions about access to support, supervision and guidance from employers and tailored development opportunities. Here's hoping you make the transition successfully.

The transition from student to qualified practitioner will continue into your first year and beyond. Just as getting your first post is the start of a longer transition, this chapter has opened up a number of issues that we will be pick up in later chapters. The first of these, Chapter 3, relates to how high quality induction, probation and supervision processes can help support you in your professional role.

Summary of key points

This chapter has introduced you to theoretical approaches to understanding the transition from a student to a newly qualified social worker. We looked at research into student work, transitions from other disciplines, and explored some of the challenges involved in making such transitions.

We have explored the concepts of sense-making (Weick, 1995) and Blair's (2000) process model for work role transition (preparation, encounter, adjustment, and stabilisation) – and hopefully you will have considered how they might apply to your own particular situation.

We have looked at the steps involved in securing your first qualified social work job, including searching for jobs, preparing applications, and starting your first job. This has included consideration of the need to challenge feelings of uncertainty, while valuing the transferability of your skills to a variety of social work settings. Case studies from a recently qualified social worker, university tutors and a manager reiterate the importance of being prepared for job interviews, and being able to demonstrate that you are up to date with current practice issues.

FURTHER READING

www.communitycare.co.uk/nqsw (accessed 24 March 2009).
This useful part of the Community Care website is informative for newly qualified social workers in that it gives a potted history of strategic developments alongside down to earth 'top tips' from managers in practice.

www.basw.co.uk (accessed 24 March 2009)
The British Association of Social Work website is not only useful for hunting down jobs (**www.baswjobs.co.uk**) but also provides a good 'links' section and updates on the status of newly qualified social workers.

www.gscc.org.uk (accessed 24 March 2009)
The regulatory body for social care in England contains useful information on becoming a social worker, including a frequently asked questions section. Click on the 'links' section to gain access to GSCC partner websites in Wales, Scotland and Northern Ireland.

Chapter 3

Managing induction, probation and supervision

Ivan Gray with contributions from Mary (NQSW) and Karen (carer)

This chapter will help you prepare for the following National Occupational Standards for Social Work.

- Key role 1, unit 1: prepare for social contact and involvement.

- Key role 5, unit 14: manage and be accountable for your own work.

- Key role 6, unit 19: work within agreed standards of social work practice and ensure own professional development.

Introduction

Do I look like a newly qualified social worker? – this was the question Mary was asked by a friend as she shopped for clothes prior to beginning her first job as a newly qualified social worker. We asked her to reflect on her first few weeks and months and the following case study gives her reflections.

CASE STUDY 3.1

Mary's first job

For me, shopping for clothes was an important part of preparing for the job and not to be underestimated! Every workplace has a different dress code. Find out what is expected from your new employer – the last thing you want is to be wearing jeans when the dress code states no denim!

Clothes aside, after finishing my degree I had a phenomenal amount of literature, research papers, journal articles and leaflets from past placements. I could hear quite clearly my lecturers saying 'how can you link research into practice?' I must admit, half of me never wanted to see those papers again. I had often read them late into the night

---

when studying for assignments, but as part of my preparation I filed any useful papers into a ring binder. This I found immensely helpful once starting the job. Access to research papers is critical with the growing culture of using research to underpin assessments.

Yet, this did not stop me experiencing losses in confidence and feelings of self-doubt in my first few weeks. My first week was very slow as I spent a lot of time in induction visits and shadowing colleagues. They would often ask for my thoughts following a visit but I would still be trying to understand the processes! I was fortunate in being given a mentor, who was always at hand to offer advice. If you can, ask your manager prior to you starting, to appoint a mentor. When you are in a busy office and everyone is saying how stressed they are, you may feel like a burden asking repeated questions. Having someone to take responsibility as your mentor, means that you can ask them questions knowing that it is okay to do so.

Working in a childcare assessment team, requires you to hit the ground running. I had been in my team about three weeks when I had acquired a large case load. I had been working for about two months when I had my first Child Protection Conference. I was seriously frightened. In an ideal world I should not have had one, but in the real world, if one of your cases reaches 'child protection' level, the likelihood is that you will have to continue working with it. My advice is to consistently and continually seek your manager's guidance and support and record all management discussions as case recordings.

I have now been in post for five months. My job is very pressured and I often start early and finish late. No day is ever the same though. And when things are good at work they are amazing . . . and long may they last!

Mary mentions her slow induction. Few newly qualified social workers appear to be given a structured induction – that is, one that helped them move into their new social work role in a clear, planned and organised fashion (Bates *et al.*, 2009). This will change, of course, with the introduction of Skills for Care (2008) and Children's Workforce Development Council (2008) pilot programmes. Nevertheless, both programmes still require that you actively manage your own induction and probation periods. This is why the first two sections of this chapter, on induction and probation, seek to provide you with models of good practice. Tailored information on supervision forms the final part of this chapter. High-quality reflective supervision is at the heart of social care, and has been and will be crucial to the success of Mary's practice, including addressing much of the emotion she talked about.

Induction

The induction of newly qualified social workers can vary considerably (Bates *et al.*, 2009). You may be warmly welcomed and provided with a well-structured, carefully planned experience that responds to your individual needs; or you may be offered a 'baptism of fire', that leaves you virtually to your own devices (Bates *et al.*, 2009). There is some consensus on the value of a good induction and its key features (Fowler, 1996; Maher *et al.*, 2003; NSWQB, 2004); good induction processes have been found to allow workers:

- to become effective more quickly;
- to settle into their teams more quickly;
- to lessen anxiety in new roles;
- to create realistic expectations of the job and the organisation;
- to reduce misunderstandings and grievances;
- to have confidence in new employers.

There is even a likely correlation between the quality of your induction and how long you stay in your new post. Fowler (1996) in an Institute of Personnel and Development (IPD) publication suggests a strong link between induction and employee retention and identifies the heavy costs to an organisation of early leavers, in other words, those who leave in the first few months of employment. Two further studies of the induction experiences of social workers (Maher *et al.*, 2003, and an Irish National Social Work Qualifications Board study (NSWQB, 2004), also note the importance of a good induction to retention. So it may well be that if you start happy you stay happy.

Good reasons abound for you viewing induction as *your* professional responsibility, accepting that a good employer should meet you more than half-way.

- Even if organisational practices do improve there will always be some posts and small organisations where a newly appointed social worker finds themselves virtually on their own with little option but to plan and manage their own induction.
- Whatever the policy initiatives, organisational practices are still likely to vary. If you have your own model of good practice you will be able build on whatever is on offer.
- Professional social workers have considerable independence and responsibility in their work. Your induction sets the foundation for the effectiveness of your future practice and needs to be managed by you from the outset.
- Induction needs to be personalised so that it responds to your needs (Bradley, 2006). This is more likely to happen if you can take control and shape it.
- It is not just a case of you fitting into the organisation; you will also be deciding if the post and the organisation is the right one for you.

This part of the chapter aims to ensure you are equipped to manage your own induction, even if organisational practices over the next few years may largely dictate your first years as a social worker.

Be clear

Be clear about what you want to achieve from your induction at the outset. This is best done by determining your aims and objectives. Aims identify the broad purpose of the activity and objectives break this down into manageable 'chunks' that help both plan and review progress.

ACTIVITY **3.1**

Spend some time thinking about your induction. What are the aims and objectives for your induction period? One way of thinking about this is to see yourself as an explorer about to enter exciting new territory. You are on a journey to find out what you need to live in this new land. Most of your exploration will consist of locating and obtaining information from the people who already live here. But it is not just an exercise in data collection – it is an emotional experience as well. You want to be accepted by the locals. You are going to work with them and will probably want them to like you and your work. In turn, they are likely to want you to respect them and their work.

See how your aim matches up with our suggested aim of induction:

To determine your role, your responsibilities and the rules, procedures, expectations and goals of the organisation you have just joined, whilst building the relationships and identifying the resources that you will need to practise effectively.

Depending on organisational practice, your induction could last just a few months or a year or more. In a broader sense, one could argue that your induction never really stops as you will be always finding out about your place of work. Nevertheless, remember the land of work is complex and well-populated. It is very common to feel overwhelmed and swamped by the number of people you meet and the amount of information you have to assimilate. Your first few days can be exhausting and chaotic. Some things might not make complete sense and you may even have doubts about how well you fit in.

Your land of work is likely to have a formal and informal culture. For instance, there will be formal procedures that say how you *should* behave and then there will be the informal ways that people *actually do* behave and get things done. This land will have some procedures you must follow so you do not put people at risk, but there is more choice than is often recognised around this essential core. It may be helpful to recognise there will not be a fixed set of people you must know or a comprehensive set of procedures identifying the *right* way to do things. Build your own view of this land and your own way of doing things.

As with most journeys into unknown lands a guide is invaluable. It might be your line manager or supervisor acts as one, working out with you who you need to see and the information you need to be given. Take any questions or clarifications to them for discussion – they might not be able to answer them immediately, but they should be able to identify others that can. You may find your guide has a structured induction plan waiting for you when you meet, clarifying your responsibilities and likely training days. If so, you may have a reduced caseload and an initial higher level of supervision, as described in the Children's Workforce Development Council (2008) pilot programme. If not, you will need to build your own induction plan, and agree it with your line manager and/or supervisor. If this is the case be mindful that corporate induction programmes tend to be very general and can too easily deteriorate into a tick-box experience. Check out what is expected and what is on offer and incorporate it into your plan. If you are managing your own induction you only need one initial contact to set the ball rolling. Once you have made contact with one key person in your network find out from them their key contacts and what they view as essential information and then locate their contacts and arrange to meet them. Gradually, by following up on these 'threads', you will identify and make contact with everyone in the network. Either way – structured or unstructured – it is important for you to take responsibility for the process and be proactive, as induction is deceptively complex – and this is why we suggest you approach it methodically.

As you chart your passage through the land it can be helpful to take notes on the information and people you come across. You should be able to find time in your first few days and weeks to think, reflect, and write notes. Keeping notes of who you meet, what they do, how you might work with them (e.g. how you make referrals), and their contact details can be invaluable. Also note any questions you have and/or points for clarification. Keeping an induction file that includes both your notes and the information you collect can help you gradually build a picture of your new land. This file can then be used as an on-going resource.

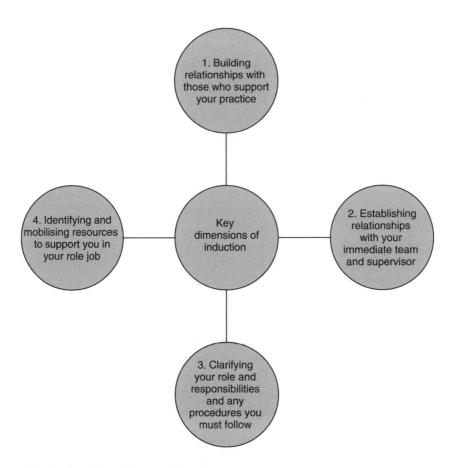

Figure 3.1 The key dimensions of induction

Just finding your way around can be important too. Some newly qualified social workers have found it helpful to buy an A–Z (or a satellite navigation tool if you can afford it) before their first day.

You will see by now that we view the process of induction as a creative space for you to fill. It is an opportunity for you to establish yourself and to shape your place in the organisation. We now explore in more detail the key dimensions of induction to help you do just that (Figure 3.1).

You can, if you wish, use these four dimensions to structure your induction file and to organise your induction plan and experience. We have broken down each key dimension into its component parts and these constitute our suggested objectives of induction that you will need to achieve in order to meet the suggested aim of induction on page 19 (Activity 3.1). We will take each of the key dimensions in turn.

Key dimension 1: building relationships with those who support your practice

1.1: to identify, make contact with and build initial relationships with those within the organisation that will support your practice

Getting to know who in the organisation makes things happen and who to go to for advice is crucial. The best source of this information is your team or others doing a similar job. Aim to meet the people they work with on a daily basis. Ask your team how they are best approached and the best way to work with them. Then methodically build up a list of people in your file, make contact with them and introduce yourself. Sometimes a telephone call is enough but with really key players you may need to go and visit them. It may pay to build a map of crucial contacts – like the one in Figure 3.2 for example. This is often

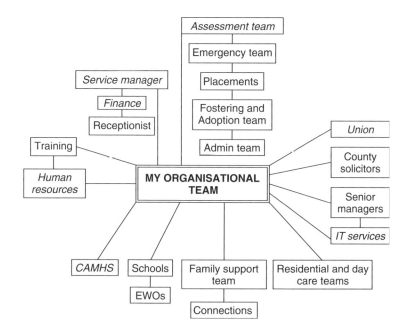

Figure 3.2 An example of a stakeholder map

called a 'stakeholder' map which is very appropriate as you are identifying all those who will have a stake in your practice and ensuring that you get to know them.

A mini-placement or shadowing can be useful for getting to know teams or sections you will work with on a daily basis, such as assessment or emergency teams. These methods can allow you to build more of a relationship that can make a big difference to the effectiveness of your work in the long term.

1.2: to identify, make contact with and build initial relationships with those outside of the organisation that support your practice

There may be as many people outside of your organisation that you will need to make contact and build a relationship with as within it. Health and social care provision is a complex network, a mixture of voluntary, independent and private sector organisations, groups and even individuals. Any care plan will inevitably demand that you mobilise this network and co-ordinate their activities.

As above, talk to your team about whom they regularly work with and ask about how to get the best from them – perhaps even what sort of problems they experience and how they get around them. If there are any formal referral mechanisms, be sure you know what they are and check on waiting times. As within your organisation, visit as appropriate any key organisations, groups and individuals and introduce yourself. Again, shadow or placement opportunities can be very valuable.

It will be essential for you to talk to people who use services and carers too. Ask colleagues for advice about people who could help. Like Karen in Case Study 3.2, they often have the best local knowledge about support and resources.

CASE STUDY 3.2

Karen's experience of meeting new social workers

G was our foster child and has lived with us for 27 years, since he was two weeks old. He has Down's Syndrome and autism as well as a serious heart condition. As such we have presented an 'interesting case' for newly qualified social workers. For a period of about 10 years, when he was younger, we had a series of them. Even when they had left us many of them would continue to ring me for advice and information for other clients. I have built a fair knowledge of local resources over the 27 years. I am always willing to be helpful but I often wonder why this sort of knowledge is not recorded somewhere central.

G loves meeting new people so it was never a problem for him to meet new social workers. He greeted everyone the same, climbing on their laps and giving them a sloppy kiss. Not all new social workers were prepared for this and had to work out how they would deal with it. One lady had very prominent teeth and G was transfixed by them and kept talking about them, much to my embarrassment, and hers. Be prepared for children to be frank and completely natural!

It was always refreshing meeting someone enthusiastic and raring to make a difference. They usually went away full of things to find out and ready to learn. The ones I appreciated most were the ones who were honest about both their own capabilities and the system within which they were working. Some promised the earth and delivered nothing. The one that impressed me the most was a lady who confessed to knowing nothing and went away on a mission to find out, always admitting when she failed and never forgetting to come back to keep me informed. She was always honest, modest and treated us as the experts in G's needs and habits.

I also remember being lectured in childcare by one new social worker. I had G and two other young children of my own. I was offended that she chose to speak to me in this way and discovered on asking that she had only a five-month-old baby! I did not appreciate her theoretical knowledge being delivered in this way. Theory is all well and good but there is nothing like a healthy respect for experience.

Key dimension 2: establishing relationships with your immediate team and supervisor

2.1: building an effective working relationship with your supervisor/s

It is worth noting at this point that at the heart of induction and probation is your interaction and relationship with your supervisor/s. In general terms the effectiveness of induction and probation, and your work generally, will be determined by the quality of your supervisory relationship. Although, good practice around managing supervision will be explored in more detail in the third and final section of this chapter (see pages 31–40), it is worth making some initial points here.

Find out about your organisation's formal supervision policy. Talk to managers about their expectations and ask colleagues for advice about what has worked (or not) for them. Try asking managers and supervisors how they like to work and establish the 'do's and don'ts'. Think about sharing a little about yourself as this can contribute to good working relationships. Tell them about what helps you most in supervision, what can cause problems for you, and pinpoint any particular learning or other needs you have. Remember this relationship will be a different relationship from the one you had with your practice educator, but it will be similar in many ways. If there is no written contract to direct your relationship, at the very least you will need to determine when you meet, how regularly and for how long – who sets the agenda, who records it, what happens if it is cancelled and how emergency situations are dealt with. Help your supervisor/s by identifying issues you wish to discuss in advance and making available any information they need. Use supervision to seek feedback on your performance and air any unhappiness and/or discontent.

Being supervised by several people, such as a team including senior practitioners, can be tough so find out how they co-ordinate activities. Try and meet middle and senior managers as well as first-line managers as their activities as a management team will impact on your work.

2.2: building effective working relationships with your immediate team

Your new team is the community of practice (Wenger, 1998) that will have the greatest impact on the effectiveness of your work and your happiness in the job. They are likely to be the greatest source of advice and support, so good working relationships with them are crucial for these reasons.

Colleagues will want to be respected by you, so make a point of seeing everyone. Even if people are busy, they usually appreciate being approached and can feel valued by you asking for their input. Start, don't finish, with your administrative and support team. They can have a considerable impact on your work and you will need to establish how to work effectively with them. Ask them directly what they like or don't like. Their personal support and goodwill can make a big difference to you in the longer term.

Find out from your social work colleagues what they are interested in and whether they have any particular specialism. Actively use their expertise, for instance, by asking your supervisor/s whose assessments are exemplary – try and get your colleagues to talk with you about what they do and don't do. And try not to forget those informal team arrangements that can assist in sustaining new relationships – they can be as simple as contributing to a tea and coffee or birthday fund (also see Chapter 6 – Joining and contributing to a team).

Key dimension 3: clarifying your role and responsibilities and any procedures you must follow

3.1: to identify and understand any legal and organisational procedures you must follow

Having up-to-date copies of essential procedures for managing situations where people can be put at risk – such as child/adult protection – is vital for safe working. You may wish to print hard copies of these procedures and put them in your induction file. Discern any discrepancies between what the procedures say and your team actually does. If in doubt, get clarification from your supervisor/s and record it.

Some procedures, for example the timing of assessments, need to be followed as they will affect performance measures that can impact on your team or organisation. As with most procedures, you will be working with others in their implementation, so it may pay to visit and discuss them with, for instance, reviewing and finance officers.

It can really be helpful to shadow people following procedures or sit in on key events such as reviews, case conferences, etc. Written procedures are much more meaningful when you see them being applied and it may pay to create your own flow diagrams for common scenarios, critical events and/or emergencies to capture the essentials. Make sure you know who the experts are, so you can approach them when things come up.

3.2: be clear about your role and responsibilities

Your job description and person specification are a good place to start in determining your role and responsibilities – your supervisor/s should be able to clarify any questions you have. Make sure you are clear about what you can or can't do and what has to be authorised by others. Use your supervisor/s and colleagues to check things out and go out of your way to share what you are doing and brief people fully.

3.3: identifying any informal rules, processes and norms that shape behaviour in the organisation alongside formal procedures and processes

To be 'at home' in your organisation you need to know not only the formal rules and regulations but also the wider culture – *the way things are done around here* – and the unwritten culture. Take notice of the small things, for example, how people answer the phone and how they explain how the system works to people who use services. These hidden informal perspectives intertwine with the formal to make up the rich tapestry of organisational life. Listen, ask, and look behind the formal espoused theory, in other words what people say they do, to the theory in use and what they actually do (Argyris and Schön, 1974). However, be slow to jump to conclusions or be over critical if things don't make sense. You may either have misunderstood or important things may just not be said openly.

3.4: understanding the goals of the organisation and how it is structured

Try to gain a broader picture of what your organisation is trying to achieve by reading business plans and service strategies. Use any corporate induction opportunities you get to speak to senior managers. It is worth remembering that the plans of other organisations may also be important to you, since your practice will in part be dependent on and impacted by their improvement plans and direction.

3.5: be confident and motivated to do the job

Getting to know your new organisation and the people in it can be traumatic and emotionally draining. It is not uncommon to have periods when you can feel a bit 'down'. You can find yourself doubting your abilities and losing confidence. These are perfectly normal reactions and they should dissipate as induction progresses.

In accepting the emotional aspects of joining an organisation, it is important to learn how to take care of yourself. Be grateful for the support people offer. Start off with 'comfortable' work you are familiar with, and enjoy transferring established skills. Move out from your comfort zone into areas of special interest over time.

Stress is an occupational hazard and workloads can easily be too high (Storey and Billingham, 2001; Gibson *et al.*, 1989). You may find that you have a protected case load, but it is important that you take responsibility for managing your workload. You may need to be realistic about what you take on and be assertive saying 'no' when you are at capacity, even if you would like to help out by taking on more. Work load management systems are never that accurate so try and establish an open dialogue with your supervisor/s about your workload. Personal 'out of work' support can be invaluable to discuss experiences and feelings but remember to keep confidentiality. Some organisations have started 'learning sets' made up of newly qualified social workers so that people can meet up to discuss their expectations and experiences. Chapter 5 of this book may also be an important resource for you as it looks at ways of managing yourself, stress and conflict.

Key dimension 4: identifying and mobilising resources to support you in your role

4.1: understanding and completing essential human resource management processes and policies

There are essential human resource management processes that have to be completed and processes that you need to know about. Often human resources personnel will find you, but if not they are usually happy to advise on the following issues:

- signing your contract and terms and conditions;
- police checks;
- hours of work and overtime arrangements;
- flexitime and time off in lieu;
- holiday entitlement and booking;
- pension arrangements;
- how you will be paid;
- discipline and grievance procedures;
- performance related pay and pay progression;
- appraisal;
- severance procedures;
- probationary period;
- equal opportunities policy;
- absence and sickness procedures;
- paternity and maternity leave.

4.2: be aware of and access welfare and support services

In most organisations welfare and support services can be important to your work-life balance. Again human resources personnel may be helpful in the following areas:

- counselling;
- employer's policies on well-being and stress;
- occupational health;
- trade union membership;
- legal advice;
- leisure activities;
- staff associations and social clubs;
- policies on 'whistle blowing'.

4.3: acquiring the essential tools and equipment you need to do the job

Having your own space and the things that you need to do the job such as a telephone, computer, diary, and stationery can be important in supporting your role and ensuring you enjoy a successful induction. Colleagues, especially administration staff, are best placed to advise you on what you will need on an everyday basis. Check out ordering procedures and what is hard to obtain, but bear in mind that colleagues will have found ways around unhelpful formal procedures.

Although it can make you feel you belong to personalise your work space, it may be that more 'flexible' working procedures and environments come with 'hot desks'. Wherever you are placed, work out where the 'heart' of team activity is, and make a point of spending some time in this environment. If you get a choice, think carefully about where you wish to sit and who you would like to sit with in the office, as it can affect your working life.

4.4: be aware and follow everyday operating procedures, including health and safety

A number of crucial procedures will be essential to the everyday operation of your organisation, including health and safety. Check out with supervisor/s and colleagues what these are for your particular organisation. They are likely to include:

- signing in and out of the office;
- logging your location and movements;
- safe interviewing procedures;
- office security;
- out of hours working and safe working procedures;
- use of IT equipment and IT assessments;
- transporting people who use services and carers;
- fire safety;
- first aid.

Find out too about everyday administrative procedures such as travel claims, allowances and receipts, timescales for arranging meetings, and computer access. Find out what these are and obtain copies of any forms you are likely to need on a daily basis. Hopefully, this gives you a useful start but you will find there is a lot to know. For instance, there will probably even be regulations to cover the gifts you may or may not receive from people who use services and carers.

4.5: access training and development opportunities and set the foundation for Continuing Professional Development (CPD)

This forms the subject of the following chapter, 'Lifelong learning, CPD, post-qualifying awards (PQ) in social work and post-registration training and learning', so only a few brief points will be made here. Your induction may include some initial or core-training workshops; for instance, basic IT training. Find out what the organisation's personal development processes are by asking team members about the best resources and which ones they use regularly. Make contact with your staff or workforce development department to find out about how to access training, book places and any cancellation procedures. Check out any on-line training and other services such as library services including the office library, help with research, and so on. Finally, you should find it helpful to share your undergraduate personal development plan with your supervisor or line manager.

ACTIVITY 3.2

Now you have read what we think induction should be about, find out from your employer all you can about the induction period and think about doing a comparison of the two – ask yourself the question, where are the gaps and how can I fill them?

Probation

Where employing organisations have probationary periods, they are usually three to six months in length – if you are unsure about the policy of your organisation, ask your line manager or human resources personnel. On the basis of this policy you will be able to determine your role within it and, as we advocate with the induction process, take responsibility for it. The experience of probationary periods of newly qualified social workers can vary considerably (Bates *et al.*, 2009) – the following aim of probation periods might therefore be helpful to you:

To jointly review and appraise with your supervisor the effectiveness of your initial practice and the suitability of the post for you; identify your future learning needs, the support you require and lay the foundation for your future performance appraisal and development planning.

ACTIVITY 3.3

Find out whether your organisation has a probationary period, and if so, what is your role within it?

It is likely that during your induction your practice and progress will be reflected upon and evaluated with your supervisor at a number of review points. It is usual that these evaluations are pulled together to make a formal judgement about your performance and conduct that is the outcome of the probationary period. It will be important for you to establish that your practice is of an appropriate standard so you will need to know how your performance will be judged, identify your development needs, and determine the support you need to work effectively. Highlight and discuss any potential issues with your supervisor or appropriate individual.

Probation has three key dimensions (Figure 3.3). We will take each in turn and explore them.

Key dimension 1: determining the job is the right one for you

A trial period works both ways. The probationary period can help you decide if the job is right for you, and the employer decide whether they think you are right for the job.

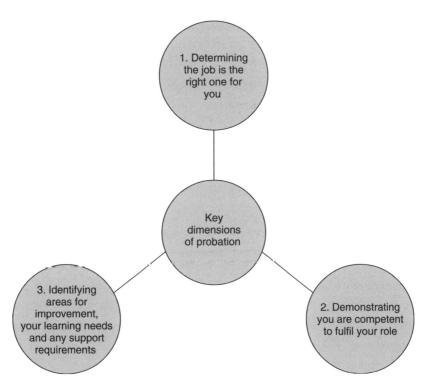

Figure 3.3 Key dimensions of probation

Dialogue is important. A good employer will want you to be open about problems in the hope of resolving them. Above all, be realistic. It will probably take up to a year to feel established in your role. However, if you decide this is not the job for you, be clear why not and what you are looking for. Discuss these issues with your supervisor and human resources personnel – there may be transfer options that could be to your benefit and that of your employer.

Key dimension 2: demonstrating you are competent to fulfil your role

The essential starting point in demonstrating your competence to fulfil your role is finding out what 'yardstick' your employer will be using to measure your performance. Your job description will usually be the first point of call but the National Occupational Standards for Social Work (Topss England, 2002), the point of reference for your qualifying training, and the GSCC (2004) codes of practice for social care workers may also be used. Make a point of asking early so there are no surprises.

It may be useful for you to review from your qualifying course your assessment and/or personal development portfolio with your supervisor/s to pinpoint your strengths and future developmental needs. Remember that identifying a development need allows you to do something about it. Again, Chapter 4 should be helpful to you in this regard.

As part of your probation period, your supervisor/s will be observing your practice, evaluating your records and reports, and listening and talking to team members and other colleagues. Although this can at times appear impressionistic, good practice is now much better defined and many managers are very good at judging performance.

It is advisable to make appraisal of your performance part of supervision and indeed a building block of your supervisory relationship. The final part of this chapter should help demystify the process of supervision. Do voice your concerns with your supervisors if there is anything you are not happy about. If other issues arise show you can take criticism 'on the nose', but make sure you are clear what the problem is and agree a way forward which should include support and help to develop your practice. These evaluations and the plans that arise from them should all be recorded in writing.

Your supervisor/s will usually initiate a series of formal review points during the probationary period where your progress is reviewed and practice that needs developing identified. There is normally a final review point and report before the probationary period is finished – in theory there should be no surprises at the end. If you have successfully completed your probationary period, you should be formally notified of this and your permanent appointment confirmed.

If your probationary period is not completed successfully your employer will follow formal procedures. Usually you will be given one verbal and two written warnings and the right to representation in meetings by a colleague, friend or union representative. Your employer must be clear about the area of your practice that is not satisfactory and provide support and access to appropriate training to bring your practice up to standard. Any probationary period can also be extended by agreement to allow you to reach these required standards. This may also happen if you are sick during the probationary period and have not had sufficient time to demonstrate your competence. If it is decided that your probationary period will not be extended you will be notified in writing and, hence, formally dismissed. The period of notice you will be given in the probation period may be less than is normally required but this is usually stated in your contract of employment.

In legal terms you cannot go to an employment tribunal on the grounds of unfair dismissal if your practice is not deemed competent at the end of the probationary period, as you will not have had twelve months continuous service. However, you may be entitled to make a claim if you have been unlawfully discriminated against and a civil action may also be possible. Employment law is complex, so if you hit difficulties in your probationary period always seek advice from human resources personnel, a trade union, the Advisory, Conciliation and Arbitration Service (ACAS) or a solicitor. These last comments are not meant to frighten you – we can only offer very broad guidance and if you need it you must make sure you take qualified specialist advice.

Key dimension 3: identifying areas for improvement, your learning needs and any support requirements

Do ask hard questions about support and development opportunities, as it is important that you are able to develop your practice and career. During any probationary and induction period the appraisal of your performance should run alongside the identification of your developmental needs and any related support requirements (see Chapter 4). Just as you should ask for feedback on your performance if this is not provided, you should also say if you are not getting the help you need to develop your practice or you do not understand what is required of you. Seek advice from human resources personnel or your trade union if this is not resolved.

It does not mean that your performance is unsatisfactory if you have learning needs. On the contrary, it is good practice to work with your supervisor/s to evaluate your practice and improve it. So even if there are areas at the end of the probationary period that still need working on, your performance can still be judged to be satisfactory. These learning needs will ideally be discussed within the process of supervision – the final section of this chapter.

Supervision

Supervision in a contended profession

Professional supervision is at the heart of social care. As the Chief Executives of Skills for Care and the Children's Workforce Development Council put it:

> *High quality supervision is one of the most important drivers in ensuring positive outcomes for people who use social care and children's services. It also has a crucial role to play in the development, retention and motivation of the workforce.*
>
> (SfC/CWDC, 2007, p 3)

Supervision is defined as:

> *An accountable process which supports, assures and develops the knowledge, skills and values of an individual, group or team. The purpose is to improve the quality of their work to achieve agreed objectives and outcomes. In social care and children's services this should optimise the capacity of people who use services to lead independent and fulfilling lives.*
>
> (SfC/CWDC, 2007, p 4)

Supervision is also a focal point where the key components of the service meet and all key activities and relationships are co-ordinated. Supervision requires commitment, respect and honesty from all participants if it is to be of benefit to the organisation and individual. Good supervision, whether it comes from your line manager or senior practitioners, will be essential to your effective practice, personal development, and welfare.

Our services and profession are by nature contested. The management of service provision necessarily involves battling with dilemmas, ambiguity, conflicting interests, incompatible expectations, value issues and judgement calls where there may not be options that can be rationally chosen as the 'best' (Healy, 2000). It is at this crucial point of co-ordination, clarification, and decision-making that these conflicts are identified and responded to. The final part of this chapter begins by exploring the nature of supervision and moves onto why it is important (including the often overlooked emotional aspects to supervision), threats to its effectiveness, and how you can evaluate the process.

ACTIVITY **3.4**

As a newly qualified social worker it is important that you take control of your own professional supervision. Think back over your previous experiences of being supervised and make some notes on:

- *what you valued most;*

- *what was least helpful;*

- *what you did to ensure that supervision was effective;*

- *what you might have done that undermined the effectiveness of supervision.*

If you can, share your thinking with your supervisor to help shape your new relationship.

Supervision as a forum for dialogue

Supervision is a crucial forum for dialogue in social care as it is where the professional and the organisation meet. In the past, professional reflection and personal development arguably dominated supervision at the expense of case and performance management to the detriment of services and professional practice. More recently, it has been argued that 'managerialism' has come to dominate supervision and that professional needs and issues have been marginalised (Jones *et al.*, 2004). However, it can be argued that supervision has never been entirely a professional domain. Supervision is also where managerial and organisational perspectives and needs meet and are resolved. Part of the tension that is endemic to supervision is competition for the space and the agenda that both you and your manager must respond to.

Managers and professionals have responsibility to ensure that there is a balance between competing but often mutual needs. The process of supervision must accommodate these needs to be effective. Figure 3.4 gives a personal illustration of your need for supervision.

There are also good grounds for approaching the process of supervision critically. If personal reflection and personal development are too easily lost from the agenda, opportunities to discuss social work values and the wider social and political effects of interventions may also be easily mislaid (Phillipson, 2002).

Time is undoubtedly a problem. It is very easy to make the shortage of it an excuse for unbalanced supervision. There is a danger that under pressure managers will undermine supervision by dominating it – rather than allowing time for exploration and reflection. What should be dealt with, and could be dealt with efficiently in formal supervision ends up being dealt with 'on the hop' in informal supervision. This often does not allow for proper communication and joint consideration of the issues. Even in assessment or emergency teams where 'on the hop' supervision is unavoidable, formal sessions are still essential.

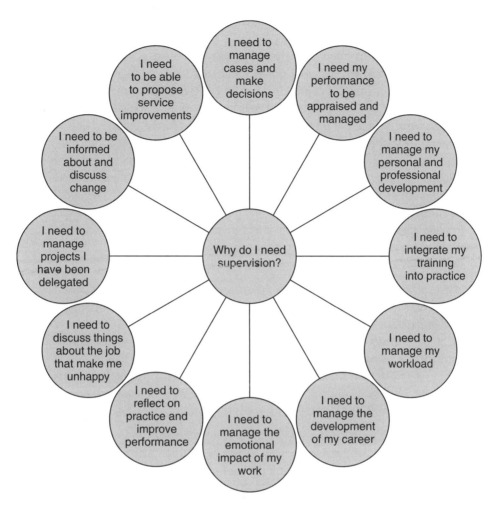

Figure 3.4 Why do I need supervision?

Supervision needs careful planning, review and plenty of time. To illustrate, one particular need in Figure 3.4 may dominate a supervision session. Future sessions may therefore need a different agenda to compensate. Keep an eye on the range of needs to ensure your supervision is balanced over time.

Supervision is likely to be your biggest training and development opportunity. Sometimes more powerful than activities such as training courses, supervision should allow you the space to ask questions, makes sense of things, and learn through your practice. With a good supervisor your personal growth and development will be enabled, and as you become more confident you will work in a more independent manner. If you are taking part in one of the new pilot schemes for newly qualified social workers you may be allo-cated an increased amount of supervision time during your induction and probationary periods (CWDC, 2008; SfC, 2008).

Emotional aspects to supervision

Whilst supervision is not counselling or therapy, it is very similar in that it requires sharing and openness, careful listening and challenge, joint problem solving and joint decision making. It also reaches for personal growth and to address the emotion that is at the heart of our work. In short, it demands a trusting and enabling supervisory relationship which of course can be very hard to achieve if in every supervision session you find yourself working with somebody different; as can happen in some teams. If you work with more than one supervisor, your manager/s will need to be active ensuring consistency of provision. You too can contribute to the effectiveness of shared supervision by recognising the difficulties it can cause, being sure to communicate as effectively as you can, and by briefing your supervisors properly. There is often opportunity to play one supervisor off against another and take advantage of breakdowns in communication and inconsistencies, so keep a reflective eye on yourself and try and be proactive in making things work. But if communication gets very difficult and issues are not being dealt with effectively, raise these issues with your manager.

Time pressures and a more procedurally driven and outcome-orientated service can mean that the culture of supervision changes to downplay the importance of emotion in our work. Managerialism is often represented as undermining the amount of supervision time devoted to the management of emotion, as well as the learning and development essential to practice. If the emotion of our work is not managed there can be a considerable impact on our effectiveness. We do not learn well if we are frightened, depressed, grieving, or frozen. Distress, if not responded to, can undermine our practice and our health (Hawkins and Shohet, 2007).

It is not just that our work involves traumatic and negative experiences, and sharing other people's grief and pain. The change process is also an emotional experience. The more fundamental the change – the more emotion (Holmes and Rahe, 1967). If you are going to be effective in improving the quality of life of carers and people who use services; if you are to respond to service changes effectively; and if you intend to develop your own practice there will be a lot of emotion about. Sometimes we might feel manipulated or frightened by the people we work with. You will need to be able to discuss these issues openly in (and outside of) supervision to ensure you remain purposeful and objective about your work.

Leadership and supervision

As a newly qualified social worker, you will be motivated to do the work you have been employed for. You will have, at least, the basic knowledge and skills to do the job. An effective manager will recognise you (like us) have a lot to learn and allow the space for you to do so. They may start by giving you lots of supervision time and guidance, gradually reducing this as they gauge the strengths and weaknesses of your practice and as you develop. You will need to play your part by taking more responsibility for your work and for supervision as time goes on.

You can use the following questions to evaluate the development of your supervision practice overtime.

- Is my supervisory relationship changing as my needs change?

- Am I working more independently over time and developing my practice, allowing my manager to delegate?

- Am I taking more responsibility for supervision, increasing my contribution and exercising more control over the process?

The effective supervision unit

The supervision standards that managers and professionals should be working to have been published recently (SfC/CWDC, 2007). It is important that you use them as the basis for your own supervisory practice. Your manager should also be using them as a point of reference, and there should be opportunity for you to evaluate your supervision with your manager. Used well, so that they lead to a genuine, shared in depth exploration of the quality of supervision, they could bring some big improvements to supervisory practice. So it is worth giving them time and attention to ensure that they do not become another 'tick-box' experience.

ACTIVITY 3.5

This is the final activity of this chapter. Use this audit tool to evaluate the supervision you receive. It has been adapted from the Skills for Care and Children's Workforce Development Council (2007) 'Providing Effective Supervision' unit of competence. There are three tables, each with a different focus. We provide a commentary on each of the performance criteria and space for your own notes.

Table 3.1 Implement supervision systems and processes

Performance criteria	Commentary	Notes
a. Implement supervision in the context of organisational policies, performance management and workforce development.	You need to locate and familiarise yourself with the organisation's supervision, appraisal, probationary and personal development policies and procedures.	
b. Develop, implement and review written agreements for supervision.	It is usual to have a supervision contract that summarises arrangements and responsibilities. They can be rudimentary, simply stating frequency, length and who has responsibility for setting them up. More complex contracts cover cancellation procedures, preparation and so on. Others may set ground rules for the relationship and identify such things as areas of interest or for personal development.	

Table 3.1 (Continued)

Performance criteria	Commentary	Notes
c. Ensure supervision records and agreed decisions are accurate and completed promptly.	You need to keep a record, at the very least, of decisions made in supervision and whoever has responsibility for recording them will need to see they are signed off. Usually it is the supervisor/s responsibility, but you should have a signed copy for your induction file or at least access to them. Areas of agreement should also be recorded.	
d. Enable workers to reflect on supervision issues and act on outcomes.	Your supervisor/s should encourage and give you space to reflect on your practice and identify your strengths, weaknesses and development needs and review you actions and care plans.	
e. Monitor and review own supervision practice and learning, reflecting on the processes and implement improvements to supervision.	There should be opportunity for you to comment on the quality of the supervision you have received. This could involve an exercise such as this one.	
f. Identify wider issues and raise them appropriately in the organisation and with other stakeholders.	Your manager or supervisor should act as a broker identifying with you practice issues that need to be picked up on in the organisation more widely, so that the quality of services can be improved.	
g. Enable access to specialist supervision, support, advice or consultation as required. Specialist supervision – can include peer, therapeutic or clinical supervision.	Specialist supervision can be an excellent way to develop your practice and can also be essential in some roles and situations which demand more support that your manager or usual supervisor/s can provide.	

Table 3.2 Develop, maintain and review effective supervision relationships

Performance criteria	Commentary	Notes
a. Create a positive environment for workers to develop and review their practice.	Supervision should challenge your practice but it should be a positive encounter that you value and where challenge is matched with encouragement and support. You should be encouraged to take responsibility and take control in reviewing and evaluating your practice.	
b. Clarify boundaries and expectations of supervision, including confidentiality.	It pays to review your previous experiences of supervision and what works or doesn't work for you. Good supervision contracts will cover these broader issues as well as clarifying confidentiality and what are (or not) suitable matters for supervision.	
c. Ensure relationships are conducted in an open and accountable way.	Both you and your supervisor/s are accountable for your practice so the relationship must be strong enough for you to share the details of your practice, including problems you are experiencing. Hidden practice can be dangerous practice.	
d. Help workers to identify and overcome blocks to performance, such as work conflicts and other pressures.	Effective practice is not just down to you. Others can influence your effectiveness in a positive fashion, as well as negatively. Chapter 5, in particular the section on dealing with conflict, may be of use here. Your supervisor/s should also be able to help with these broader issues.	
e. Assist workers to understand the emotional impact	It is a tough job – one that can affect us all deeply. The	

Table 3.2 (Continued)

Performance criteria	Commentary	Notes
of their work and seek appropriate specialist support if needed.	emotion of your work needs to be on the agenda for the sake of your own health, but also because it can impact on your practice. Some people who use services can be manipulative or frightening – openness about their impact on you will help ensure your practice is purposeful and objective.	
f. Ensure the *duty of care* is met for the well-being of workers.	Your employer has responsibility for your health and safety including safe working arrangements outside of the office, stress and workload balance.	
g. Recognise diversity and demonstrate *anti-discriminatory practice* in the supervision relationship.	Supervision should respond to your individual needs and actively seek not to discriminate against you.	
h. Give and receive constructive **feedback** on the supervisory relationship and supervision practice.	Both you and your supervisor/s need to reflect on and discuss the quality of your supervision and aim to improve it over time.	
i. Audit and develop own skills and knowledge to supervise workers, including those from other disciplines when required.	Your manager should be seeking to develop their skills as a supervisor. You can help them do this by giving them positive and constructive feedback, identifying areas where supervision can be improved. Having good supervisory practice on the agenda is also useful as the supervision of others will become one of your responsibilities as your career progresses.	

Table 3.3 Develop, maintain and review practice and performance through supervision

Performance criteria	Commentary	Notes
a. Ensure workloads are effectively allocated, managed and reviewed.	It is very difficult to come up with a definitive workload management system that determines fair workloads for all, as your work will be too complex and variable to be easily categorised and measured. Good dialogue that regularly addresses what you are being allocated, how, and whether it is manageable, is essential.	
b. Monitor and enable workers' competence to assess, plan, implement and review their work.	Your performance as a case manager should not only be evaluated, but there should be opportunities for you to develop and improve it.	
c. Ensure supervisor and workers are clear about accountability and the limits of their individual and organisational authority and duties.	Induction and supervision are the best places to clarify any areas of confusion that can arise. Job descriptions and procedures are often not definitive – discussion works.	
d. Ensure workers understand and demonstrate *anti-discriminatory practice.*	Your qualifying course will have given a lot of attention to this topic, but do not let it drift – make it an explicit feature of your supervision agenda.	
e. Ensure work *with people who use services* is outcomes-focused and that their views are taken account of in service design and delivery.	Work with individuals needs to be achieving outcomes agreed with them. Supervision also needs to address the broader development of services and service quality and people who use services can be involved in this.	
f. Identify risks to users of services and workers and take appropriate action.	Risks need to be clearly identified, methodically assessed and actions agreed to manage them effectively. Any assessment and agreed plans should be recorded.	

Table 3.3 (Continued)

Performance criteria	Commentary	Notes
g. Obtain and give timely feedback on workers' practice, including feedback from people who use services.	Both you and your supervisor have a responsibility to evaluate your practice and improve it. Actively seeking feedback on your performance (especially from people who use services and carers) and discussing and acting on it is a joint responsibility.	
h. Identify learning needs and integrate them within development plans.	It is important that you are clear about what areas of your practice you want to develop. Make sure your learning objectives and development plans are focused on these needs.	
i. Create opportunities for learning and development.	You should be offered and take opportunity to make use of a range of on and off the job development opportunities. Their effectiveness in meeting your needs should be evaluated.	
j. Assess and review performance, challenge poor practice and ensure improvements in standards.	Supervision should encompass appraisal. Your performance should be evaluated jointly against agreed standards on the basis of readily identified evidence. The evaluation and agreed improvement plans should be recorded together with any differences of opinion.	
k. Enable multi-disciplinary, integrated and collaborative working as appropriate.	This is essential to service quality and demands regular review and evaluation. Chapter 6 of this book will no doubt help here as multidisciplinary working is an essential element of practice. Many quality problems originate here and many quality improvements lie with more effective multi-agency and collaborative working.	

Summary of key points

- Your period of induction will be crucial in determining your role and responsibilities and the rules, procedures, expectations and goals of the organisation you have just joined.

- High quality reflective supervision is at the heart of social care and will be crucial to the success of your future practice.

- Use current standards to evaluate the quality of your induction period and supervision processes.

FURTHER READING

Hawkins, P and Shohet, R (2007) *Supervising in the helping professions*. 3rd edn Bucks: Oxford University Press.

This is a classic, thoughtful, easy to read text that offers a balanced view of supervision and recognises the needs and the importance of the whole person to social work practice. Combine it with the good practice model provided by the SfC/CWDC (2007) Supervision Unit and you will have a useful supervision toolkit.

Kadushin, A and Harkness, D (2002) *Supervision in social work*. 4th edn New York: Columbia University Press.

This is an excellent review of social work supervision that not only addresses the function of social work supervision but also potential problems.

Chapter 4

Lifelong learning, continuing professional development, post-qualifying awards and post-registration training and learning

Steven Keen, Di Galpin, Lynne Rutter, Keith Brown and Graham Ixer with contributions from Angela (NQSW) and Jane (social worker)

This chapter will help you to meet the following National Occupational Standard for Social Work.

- Key role 6, unit 19: work within agreed standards of social work practice and ensure own professional development.

You are never too old to learn

The phrase *you are never too old to learn* is exactly what the concept of Lifelong Learning is all about (Commission for European Communities (CEC), 2007).

> *Learning one set of skills at school, technical college or university is no longer enough to carry people throughout their working life. But there is one basic skill that is becoming increasingly important in today's fast-changing technological universe: being able to learn and adapt to the new skills and training that will be required.*

> (OECD, 2007, p 1)

The concept of Lifelong Learning is here to stay and will continue to be a widely held policy object among the Organisation for Economic Co-operation and Development (OECD) countries, not least in the UK where the amount of bodies and agencies working in this, learning and skills, system is breathtaking.

There is little difference between the concepts of Lifelong Learning and Continuing Professional Development (CPD). CPD emphasises the importance of personal development to professional practice in particular, but is not just confined to education and qualifications – it embraces any learning activity. CPD also emphasises that learning is the responsibility of the professional and like Lifelong Learning recognises the importance of the effectiveness of professionals as learners and their commitment to learning as the only constants in an otherwise fast changing world – one where today's skills and understanding may not meet tomorrow's tasks. CPD has as its ultimate outcome the improvement of services and can start with the question *what kind of service do we want to deliver?* (Skinner, 2005, p 14).

To deliver these services the government has outlined its drive to ensure the social services workforce is appropriately qualified and regulated (DH, 1998). *Modernising the Social Care Workforce* (Topss England, 2000) and the *Skills for Care Workforce Planning Toolkit* (Topss England, 2004) provide guidance for employers in developing strategies to meet these aims. Galpin (2009, p 67) notes that:

> *professional development has focused on the requirements of employers (e.g. Topss England, 2002; GSCC, 2004) In regulated services to support workforce planning and analysis to meet a range of national requirements.*

CPD is a planned process that contributes to both service and professional development. Within this process there are three key groups who need to work in partnership to fulfil their responsibilities to ensure workers are adequately educated and trained to deliver high quality services: the individual, employers, and providers of CPD. Each has different responsibilities.

The individual's are:

- to take a proactive approach in formulating and engaging in learning activities;
- to ensure they meet professional registration requirements.

The employer's are:

- to meet workforce planning requirements to ensure the service is able to fulfil its statutory duties;
- to support individuals in meeting professional registration requirements;
- to support individuals in their pursuit of CPD; this may include financial, study leave, and mentoring opportunities.

The provider's are:

- to provide CPD activity that meets individual needs and the needs of employers;
- to ensure CPD activity enables learning and professional development.

But what does this mean for the newly qualified social worker?

This chapter is not focused on employers and the delivery of services – Chapter 7 is though. Instead, the focus of this chapter is on *you*, and on where *you* want to be professionally in one to five years time. If you have never considered this spend some time now thinking about your response and on the next activity. Angela's case study should be helpful as you deliberate on where you want to be professionally in the coming years, and in particular, discern how CPD, PQ awards and Post-Registration Training and Learning (PRTL) – the main sub-divisions of this chapter – can support your likely career choices.

CASE STUDY 4.1

Where do I want to be in a few years time? Angela's story

I was told I could answer this question honestly so . . . in a few years time, I would like to be sitting on a tropical beach with my loved ones, remembering fondly the days when I used to be in social work! By then, the numerous excuses as to why I should not do the PQ award will all have been exhausted and I won't be struggling through the last unit of the course whilst trying to balance working, eating, sleeping and family life. On a serious note, having thought about the concept of Lifelong Learning, it is helpful to consider where I have come from in order to try and answer the question, where do I want to be in a few years time?

The path to becoming a social worker began when I started work as an administrator for Social Services and was then encouraged to do the new social work degree. Prior to this I had studied for three years to obtain a degree in social sciences. It all sounds nicely academic, but apart from the placements I had little experience of actually doing the job and the thought of doing any more 'official' studying, has deterred me at present from pursuing any PQ awards.

However, since getting my first job as a newly qualified social worker, my knowledge and experience have obviously increased. I have found that I quickly started to engage in an almost constant flow of learning and development coming from various different sources such as classroom-based trainers, people who use services, other colleagues, line managers and so on. This knowledge has helped me on a personal and professional level, which in turn has had a positive affect on my practice.

I have found the internal training courses provided within my authority especially helpful as they seem to be able to balance knowledge along with practical application. They also count towards the PRTL study days required by the General Social Care Council.

*Alongside this, I have had the opportunity to follow a slightly hazy (at present) interest in social work research and have applied to train as a mentor/possible teacher through the Pass on Your Skills Course (**www.passonyourskills.com**). These are two specific areas of interest to me and may actually provide part of the answer as to where I want to be in a few years time.*

There seems to be a number of opportunities now for social workers to pursue a wide variety of interests and if you are unsure of where you want to be then my advice would be to not be afraid to experiment, for instance, by shadowing colleagues until you find something that fits with you.

At the end of the day, I want to be the best social work practitioner that I can be. I realise now more than ever that in order to achieve this, it will not be a 'one off' event. It is much more of a journey that requires a commitment to engage with the process of Lifelong Learning in whatever form that takes.

ACTIVITY 4.1

- *Think about what you are good at and what you like to do.*

- *Think about where you want to be, or where you want to work, in one to five years time.*

- *Think about what skills and knowledge you would like to develop during this time.*

Please feel free to revisit your undergraduate professional development plan.

Continuing professional development

Recognition of the need for social work practitioners to engage in learning activities has increased in the UK since the early 1990s, as government, employers, and employees have identified the need for CPD (Pietroni, 1991; DH, 1998). Long-standing evidence in a range of industries shows that accessible career pathways and workforce development opportunities are critical in retaining staff and creating a motivated and stable workforce (Parker and Whitfield, 2006; Skinner, 2005). Today, many discussions around CPD focus on these economic and/or political arguments. Put another way, vocational learning helps meet targets designed to ensure the workforce is suitably qualified. Yet, this viewpoint tends to overshadow the personal and socially transformative aspects of participating in CPD. CPD makes complete sense in many ways – it has its own rewards for the individual as well as organisations. *But often the individual is forgotten*. This is why we view CPD as a three-way responsibility between employers, those prescribing and providing the learning opportunities and, you, the practitioner. By working together collaboratively, tensions can be managed by allowing reciprocal advice and support to meet one another's needs in the ever-changing world of social work (see Brown *et al*., 2006, pp 7–30, for guidance on how to manage these partnerships).

Times of change can result in greater strain and stress, as well as offering good opportunities for development. The world of social work and social care is no stranger to change. In recent years, we have witnessed a raft of new legislation and associated organisations in our sector that have changed both the practice and role of social workers in addition to providing the strategic impetus for CPD to become an integrated part of this world. The following are examples in England:

- Set up in 2001, the Social Care Institute for Excellence (SCIE) develops and promotes knowledge about good practice in social care.

- The General Social Care Council (GSCC), established under the Care Standards Act 2000, regulates standards for the social care workforce.

- The Care Quality Commission (formerly the Commission for Social Care Inspection (CSCI), the Commission for Health Inspectorate and the Mental Health Act Commission).

- In 2005, Topss England split to become Skills for Care and CWDC. Part of the new UK-wide Sector Skills Council for social care – known as Skills for Care and Development, Skills for Care supports adult social care employers in improving care provision. CWDC, the Children's Workforce Development Council, set up in 2005, is an employer-led organisation ensuring that people working with children have the best possible training, qualifications, support and advice.

• Skills for Care (2006a) launched its CPD strategy in 2006 and, more recently, CWDC has begun its three-year business plan (2008–11). The Department of Health has very recently launched its workforce strategy for adult social care in England (DH, 2009).

Practice can become routine as you forget why you came into the profession in the first place. This is why it is important to consider why you might engage in CPD. Learning new things can make us more aware of the gaps in our knowledge and skills. Think about driving; would you pass your driving test if you took it tomorrow? Probably not . . . over the years we will have picked up bad habits, but these will not have stopped us from, for example, driving to work. Practice is a bit like this – how many bad habits do we pick up along the way, when we continue to work in the same way, day in day out?

ACTIVITY 4.2

In his book about England's rise to Rugby World Cup glory, head coach, now Sir Clive Woodward, tells the story of how he prepared his squad for thinking in detail (Woodward and Potanin, 2004, pp 165–7). Using an exercise from organisational consultant Humphrey Walters he asked his players to look at the sentence in capitals below, and tell him how many F's they saw within it – take about 30 seconds and do the same.

FINISHED FILES ARE THE RE-
SULT OF MANY YEARS OF SCIENTIF-
IC STUDY COMBINED WITH THE
EXPERIENCE OF MANY YEARS

When we, the authors, did this exercise for the first time, we all saw three F's. Studies show that 95 per cent of people will only see three F's (Woodward and Potanin, 2004, p 166) – the F's in FINISHED, FILES and SCIENTIFIC. In actual fact there are six F's. We so take for granted the word 'OF' that our brains have learned to filter it out of our vision. The point of including this task is this – what do we take for granted in the way we practise? In our everyday work, what do we filter out so that we no longer see it? Sometimes the act of just stopping and thinking about our practice can bring about some interesting results.

What is CPD?

CPD can be defined as a continuous, planned, learning and development process that contributes to work-based learning and personal development, and can be applied or assessed against competences and organisational performance (Skills for Care, 2006a). As such, it is any activity that contributes to lifelong learning and is represented diagrammatically as shown in Figure 4.1. CPD can be a managed process supported by organisational policy and procedures, but it is best if you are able to take responsibility for it. CPD, therefore, applies to all levels of workers and managers and has as its outcome the improvement of services. In very broad terms, CPD consists of two main types of provision.

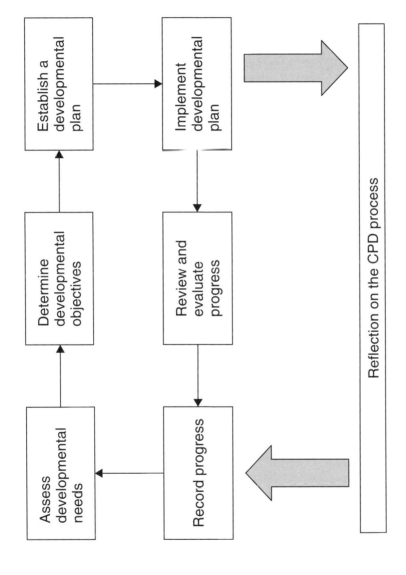

Figure 4.1 The CPD process

Formal learning – leading to recognised awards and qualifications, in-house workshops, induction.

Informal learning – such as action learning sets, self-directed learning, online learning, job swaps, quality circles, mentoring, shadowing and buddying.

CPD is therefore varied and not just confined to training and/or qualifications. In other words, CPD will not always be provided via a course or programme. The implication is that not all development opportunities have to go upwards. Skinner (2005, p 9) uses a wonderful climbing frame analogy to show that people can still develop professionally, even if learning opportunities are offered at different levels, by moving sideways rather than vertically. For instance, vertical progress will happen when individuals undertake PQ awards as they will be acquiring new skills and knowledge, possibly for new, more responsible positions; whereas horizontal personal development will happen when people consolidate or update their competence (professionalism and lifelong learning) but maintain their existing position.

Key building blocks are needed to underpin, develop and sustain this type of CPD provision – ranging from effective staff supervision and appraisal systems, succession planning, practice learning, clear leadership and management roles, to an embedded organisational culture of learning (Parker *et al.*, 2006). Enthusiasts are needed at a local level to champion CPD, and flexible learning methods alongside monetary and responsibility-related incentives are also important. Perhaps one of the main underpinning features is the necessity of evaluating all CPD, whether it occurs within a formalised programme or not. Career structures should recognise and reward all types of staff progression and development, but this in turn should be based on appropriate evidence. We believe that all CPD should be evaluated and we show later how a framework for critical thinking and reflection may aid this 'evidencing' process.

You can see that at whatever level CPD is being undertaken, or however it is being done, it will be about developing practice in some way and measuring this development. In many ways, it is only when you commence work and operate as a qualified social worker that you begin to reflect on your learning and experience to date, and begin to realise what you do not know. So, CPD is vital in order to give you the opportunity to reflect and consolidate your learning to date and to plan your development. To this end, the appendices in this book cover a number of areas that newly qualified social workers highlight they need development in – be they assessment, court or writing skills, care management and contracting, child protection or PQ awards – please use them as appropriate.

Knowing how you learn can also help you learn. Honey and Mumford (2008) are best known for their learning-styles questionnaire. Knowing your learning style can not only accelerate your learning, as you carry out activities that fit your learning style, but also prevent you from making mistakes (Swinton, 2008). One simple example is, if you know that you tend to act without thinking then you can consider spending time reflecting on experiences before taking decisions (Swinton, 2008). Honey and Mumford consider there are four types of individual – activists, reflectors, theorists and pragmatists. Activists, as the name suggests act first, consider the consequences later and immerse themselves fully in new experiences. Reflectors are more cautious, tend to step back and can be slow to reach conclusions. Theorists think through problems in a logical manner whilst pragmatists are impatient with endless discussion and often act quickly and confidently on ideas. If you have not already, please consider completing the learning styles questionnaire (available from **www.peterhoney.com**) to help you discern your learning style.

Reflecting on your practice as well as your learning style is also useful. Most professional bodies agree that the notion of CPD is inextricably linked with critically reflective practice, and so include the notion of capability as well as competence in order to deal with the complexity, uncertainty and ever changing nature of social work. In this respect, Postle *et al.* (2002, p 159) argue for an inclusive approach to CPD, seeing competent practitioners as continuing to '*develop skills and knowledge in a non-linear, reflective process, converting practice into praxis in their interrelation of theory and its application*'. Similarly, Preston-Shoot (2000, p 92) shows that '*competent practitioners should be confident, credible, critical and creative*'. From our experience of social work education, although we live at a time when evidence-informed practice is frequently talked about, we repeatedly hear that workers usually do not have the time to consult the evidence to inform their practice. Indeed, some report they do not know where to go and find the evidence let alone use it. Therefore, opportunities for CPD have a great benefit in providing a focus for you to locate evidence and to critically reflect on your practice.

Critical thinking and reflection for CPD

Reviewing and reflecting on practice is important for developing competence and capability. Rolfe *et al.* (2001) show that developing practice and learning cannot be separated. The development of practice is a lifelong activity; it generates experiential knowledge and so to practise is also to learn. The use of personal learning plans or portfolios (Skills for Care, 2006a; Hull *et al.*, 2004) can be an effective way to achieve and evidence such learning. For many it leads to insights and new understandings. However, reviewing and developing practice can also be threatening and provoke anxiety. It is hard work, involving self-doubt and mental blocks. Professional knowledge comprises theoretical knowledge and experience, as well as the understanding of process – these are complex ideas to deal with. Critical thinking and reflection on practice, therefore, can be invaluable tools to review, consolidate, and develop practice because they provide the necessary guidance and instructive frameworks associated with experiential learning; with personal learning plans or portfolios; and with producing robust evidence of such learning. Learning Matters texts like *Critical Thinking for Social Work* (Brown and Rutter, 2006, 2008) aim to support and develop this process and the following ideas are adapted from these books as a proposed model of how to evidence CPD.

What is critical thinking and reflection?

Critical thinking and reflection are processes that allow you to think back on experience more deeply and 'drill down' to identify relevant underpinning knowledge (experiential and theoretical) and values, as well as the deliberations and judgements that make up your expertise. Not only this, they allow a more questioning and creative approach – highlighting different options, alternatives or implications that could inform and help you develop future practice – thereby ensuring that CPD does what it says on the tin, in other words it continues in time, adopts a professional approach and is developmental.

Why critically think and reflect?

Critical thinking and reflection should not produce cynics but practitioners aware of the reality of practice, who are committed, well-informed, rational, and supported by relevant and valid skills and knowledge. These 'critical practitioners' will be the type of staff people using social care services need to meet their needs and who they can trust and respect. On a day-to-day level, there are dangers associated with the development of expertise in practice. As we have tried to demonstrate earlier with the, how many F's exercise, any practice can easily fall into purely intuitive and routine methods because they are safer and less time-consuming. We sometimes develop rules of thumb and standardise our approaches to problems in order to survive our workloads. However, these habitual practices are more difficult to keep under critical control and tend not to adapt easily to new circumstances. Using critical thinking and reflection to develop professional expertise will take you beyond repeating the same experience or implicitly developing your own implicit 'rules of thumb'. Rather, you can explore and understand your practice deliberations, decisions, and actions in meaningful ways and develop new perspectives for future practice using available theory, research, knowledge, and experience. The main outcome will be an evaluation of the learning and development pertaining to future practice: the development of self as a critical practitioner (Adams *et al.*, 2002). The aim is to get you to think beyond the acknowledgement and description of feelings, or the elements of a particular situation, to an evaluation of how you dealt with it and the resulting decisions and actions relevant to values as well as future practice methods.

How can it be achieved?

Critical thinking and reflection can be triggered by the recognition of something not 'normal' – possibly an unexpected action or outcome (positive as well as negative) or an intuitive feeling of unease. Supervision can be used to pick up on and explore these situations, and your supervisor may be able to spot and challenge unhelpful practice. There are real benefits in keeping up-to-date in a professional area of practice and having the necessary critical skills. Such a practitioner will have more knowledge and awareness to recognise incidents for what they are and have more self-confidence to deal with them explicitly. Initially, frameworks to help critical reflection can be used to guide further thought and exploration. Table 4.1 will enable you to link various aspects of practice to certain critical thinking activities, to demonstrate and develop critical practice for CPD.

Use the left-hand side of Table 4.1 to identify the relevant aspects of practice you want to explore and then move across to the right-hand column to see which particular critical thinking activities are likely to support them. By understanding and discussing practice in these terms, you can more readily articulate your competence, notice where further development is necessary and see where extra training or education is appropriate to support development. For example, you may have relevant knowledge about recent Deprivation of Liberty legislation (DH, 2005) but realise you now need more information about the specific implications of this legislation and how to apply it. To find such information may require further reading or training.

Table 4.1 Elements and activities of critical 'expert' practice

Practice experience	Critical thinking activities
Developing knowledge	Integrating values and experience
	Holding views based on valid evidence but seeking and accepting relevant but alternative viewpoints and perspectives
	Keeping up-to-date, reading and researching
	Identifying and challenging own and others' assumptions
	Recognising and questioning viewpoints and arguments
Assessment of situations in depth; selection and adoption of a framework that fits	Understanding when more information and input is required, knowing where and how to get it
	Gaining alternative perspective/s or reframing a situation
	Lateral, creative thinking and/or problem solving
Leads to action	Decision-making and planning; use of discretion; responsibility and risk assessment
	Seek out and take proper account of all stakeholders' input
	Thinking through implications
	Predict possible outcomes and allow for alternatives
Monitoring progress and evaluating outcomes	Formulate clear aims and objectives at the start, getting feedback, making judgements and reviewing progress.
	Prepared to adapt, change and learn where necessary

Adapted from Brown and Rutter (2006, pp 38–39), and Brown and Rutter (2008, p 45)

The next practical task offers you a series of progressive steps to think critically about a practice experience (see Table 4.2). As such it demonstrates that there are multiple dimensions to critical reflection.

Identify a practice experience you wish to think more critically about. Start by thinking about the main descriptive details and use the examples and questions in Table 4.2 to guide you. Then work on this material by identifying, analysing and evaluating the key points and issues, the input and the outcomes, and finally draw out the learning from this evaluation and show how it can affect or impact on practice. So, there is an evaluated conclusion (i.e. something that can be appropriately assessed) in terms of your understanding and learning and development. This is the key purpose of CPD, especially if you are not undertaking a formal course.

Table 4.2 Dimensions of critical reflection

Dimensions	Example
Description Be aware of important and relevant aspects of self and the situation – including your feelings and thoughts concerning complex issues and dilemmas.	For example, if you were reflecting on a home visit, you might consider the details concerning your role, the situation of the person you were visiting and their feelings, how you prepared for the visit and the timing of it. What were you feeling? What do you want to achieve?
Critical analysis Now think about your feelings, actions and decisions. Challenge or question any underlying assumptions, knowledge, experience, etc., and try to become more objective.	Using the same example how well do you think you communicated? Why did you use particular techniques during the visit? How was this visit different from previous ones? Are the differences significant? What were your assumptions? What were your objectives and why?
Evaluation Now review the processes and outcomes.	Again using the same example, perhaps consider how well you think the relationship is developing – is there anymore information you think you might help e.g. what are the risks and do you think they can be managed effectively? And are there other ways you could have handled this situation? How well did you meet your objectives? How relevant, suitable or appropriate were your knowledge, objectives or decisions etc?
Learning Finally, consider the learning that has come from this reflection and how you might share it.	What does this mean for your practice? A consideration of the above could lead you to ideas for future practice, both in terms of your own learning needs and improvements in service provision. How has this changed your thinking?

Adapted from Brown and Rutter (2006, p 19) and Brown and Rutter (2008, p 24).

Both of these frameworks (Tables 4.1 and 4.2) can be used within supervision sessions, self-directed learning activities or in association with a formal course. They can also be used as tools to demonstrate the learning associated with CPD, especially for the Consolidation and Preparation for Specialist Practice part of the new PQ Specialist Social Work Award, and as discussed later on in this chapter, Post-Registration Training and Learning.

Regardless of the quality of CPD provision and support structures, only you, however, can provide the motivation to learn. Admittedly, that motivation may be based on external factors such as monetary reward, but more often than not it may be based on a desire to make a difference in the lives of vulnerable people. Developing your own practitioner-centred approach to CPD is important. The first activity in this CPD sub-section encouraged you to think about what skills you would like to develop in the next few years. This final activity will cause you to think further about the five key subject areas we have covered so far in this chapter and your own approach to CPD.

ACTIVITY 4.4

How might you develop a personalised and meaningful approach to CPD? Here are some topic areas and related questions to reflect on.

- *The context of CPD: are you clear why you are participating in CPD? Is it all about registration, job chances, improving job satisfaction or service outcomes for people who use services? Is it about improving your work environment or supporting others in the workplace?*

- *Partnership: who is involved in your likely CPD partnerships? What are these partnerships like and how can they be improved?*

- *Motivation: what is your motivation to learn? What factors might improve your motivation to learn in the future?*

- *Learning styles: how do you best learn? How you can incorporate this learning style into CPD activity?*

- *Reflection: are you able to stop and reflect on practice? What barriers stop this process? How might you remove or lessen these barriers?*

At this point it might be useful for you to draw up an action plan. Within the plan, include a timeline, a list of key partnerships you might like to develop and how, and other activities you could engage in. It is likely that PQ awards will be on your action plan and it is to this formal CPD provision we now turn.

PQ framework

England (General Social Care Council), Scotland (Scottish Social Services Council), Wales (Care Council for Wales) and Northern Ireland (Northern Ireland Social Care Council) have their own regulatory bodies for social work and social care. They have been given the remit of developing national CPD pathways to meet employers' and practitioners' needs (e.g. for England see Skills for Care, 2006a). Whilst the focus of this chapter is on England, a brief overview will provide you with a broader understanding of the development of PQ awards in social work across the UK.

The revised PQ framework came into force on 1 September 2007 (GSCC 2005a). This revised framework builds on the previous one and aims to develop the quality of social work practice. The framework is geared to assist you, the practitioner, in a world of practice where learning becomes experiential, in the widest sense of the word, and for many, much more real. Expertise is now developed as theoretical knowledge and understanding tried out in unique, real-life cases where judgements are made in uncertain and complex situations.

There are three levels within the revised PQ framework:

- specialist;

- higher specialist;

- advanced.

Each of the above levels corresponds to different stages of professional development. Each level is modular i.e. the curriculum is broken down into more distinct modules of study (Higher Education Policy Institute (HEPI), 2004) and able to be accessed by appropriately qualified individuals from other professions (GSCC, 2005a). Every programme approved by the care councils is linked to a regional or national planning and commissioning process, within the context of broader workforce planning and development. For example, the Scottish Social Services Council (SSSC) has developed the standards and requirements for specialist training for social workers within the context of a development plan that covers the whole of the social care workforce in Scotland (SSSC, 2005). The Care Council for Wales has developed an all Wales approach, in collaboration with employers, to link specific PQ modules and other courses to specific posts and career progression (Higham, 2006). In Northern Ireland, the Northern Ireland PQ Education and Training Partnership is responsible to the Northern Ireland Social Care Council (NISCC) for the development of the framework, its accreditation and assessment – the framework draws on both academic and professional pathways to CPD (NISCC, 2006). Indeed, in Scotland, Wales, and Northern Ireland the PQ framework is linked to academic awards and professional pathways to achieve CPD. Yet, in England, the PQ framework is solely linked to higher education at both undergraduate and postgraduate level.

Not all Higher Education Institutions will offer all three levels of award. Within your organisation, the revised framework should be linked to supervision, appraisal and performance management, and key stages of ongoing professional development. Find out more information from your care council, employer and higher education institute (HEI) on what they offer.

ACTIVITY **4.5**

Look at your care council's website to find out more about CPD pathways and the PQ framework.

*England – **www.gscc.org.uk***

*Scotland – **www.sssc.uk.com***

*Wales – **www.ccwales.org.uk***

*Northern Ireland – **www.niscc.info** or **www.nipqetp.com***

Then find out from your intended university or workforce development team what PQ programmes they offer.

Find out how PQ programmes are linked to supervision, appraisal and performance management within your organisation.

Before you decide how these programmes might fit into your plans for the future, read on a bit further about the nature of specialist, higher specialist, and advanced levels.

PQ Award in Specialist Social Work

Specialist awards focus on the knowledge and skills needed for consolidating, extending and deepening initial professional competence. The consolidation of competence in a specialist context is the focus of a single module located at the first stage of this programme – it is usually called the 'Consolidation and Preparation for Specialist Practice' unit. We believe that the consolidation module should be considered the basis of CPD for all newly qualified social workers – certainly at Bournemouth University the consolidation unit has been designed to meet GSCC (2005), CWDC (2008) and Skills for Care (2008) outcomes and act as a bridging unit from qualifying to practice. To complete the PQ award in Specialist Social Work practitioners need to demonstrate competence in thinking critically about improving their own practice and self-management, their direct work with people who use services, families and carers, and their supervision, mentoring, teaching, and assessment of others. There are a number of pathways to achieve the specialist award after the consolidation unit:

- social work with children, young people, their families and carers;

- social work with adults;

- leadership and management.

The minimum academic level for the specialist award is at Level H. Level H is equivalent to the standard required in the final year of an undergraduate or honours degree. For those who already have a social work degree, the main outcome from a specialist award will usually be a 120 Level H credit graduate diploma. Credits are simply a means of attaching academic value or currency to modules (HEPI, 2004).

PQ Award in Higher Specialist Social Work

In England, the PQ Award in Higher Specialist Social Work was created by the General Social Care Council for areas of work it considered unsuitable for a specialist level. It focuses on the knowledge and skills needed for making complex judgments and to discharge high levels of responsibility for the co-ordination of social support and the management of risk. Practitioners need to develop complex problem solving skills, along with a high level of critical thinking, reflection and analysis. There are five areas of practice in which you can achieve the Higher Specialist Award:

- social work with children, young people, their families and carers;

- social work with adults;

- mental health;

- practice education;

- leadership and management.

The Higher Specialist Award is studied at Level M or Master's level, and usually for a postgraduate diploma (PG diploma or 120 Level M credits).

PQ Award in Advanced Social Work

This award focuses on the advanced knowledge and skills needed for professional leadership and the improvement of services at a strategic level. As such the programme concentrates on the capacity to develop and undertake research and on professional mastery of a specific area of work, with a strong emphasis on various aspects of professional leadership; that is, leadership in relation to practice management, education, or applied research. This level is equivalent to the standard required for a Master's degree, that is, at Level M, and is usually a full Master's degree award comprising a postgraduate diploma (120 credits) and a dissertation (60 credits).

PQ options

You have a number of PQ options depending on your plans for your future. The choices you make will depend on a variety of factors including:

- what you want;

- what your employer expects;

- what your professional regulatory body requires of you.

When deciding which route to follow please do not automatically dismiss specialist level awards because you already have a degree. PQ is primarily about consolidating and developing practice competence and skills in your *specialist* area of practice. Whilst your previous studies will have enabled you to obtain the necessary generic knowledge and qualifications to become a social worker, you may have begun to notice the application of generic learning to your specialist area of practice is not always straightforward. The phrase *if I knew then what I know now* comes to mind when we think about the assignments we wrote before we became full-time practitioners.

Here are five brief scenarios of PQ routes for newly qualified social workers.

I work in childcare, what can PQ offer me?

You may have options for PQ study at all three levels – specialist, higher specialist and advanced. It depends on what is on offer in your area. For instance, some universities will offer a specialist award to enable you to consolidate your academic learning with professional experience in your specialist area of practice. Higher specialist and advanced awards are likely to become more common in the future and offer a route at a higher level of academic study, for example, master's degree. Please note that some awards have a very specific focus, for example, on fostering and adoption. Is this what you want?

I work with adults, what can PQ offer me?

You may have options for PQ study at all three levels – specialist, higher specialist and advanced. However, as we write, it appears that most universities are offering this award just at the specialist level. This award will help you consolidate learning in your specialist area of practice, and also enable you to meet the Department of Health's (DH) requirements for a Best Interest Assessor in the context of Deprivation of Liberty Safeguards under the Mental Capacity Act 2005 (DH, 2005). This is a useful additional qualification in terms of practice, but also in terms of career progression and seeking other jobs.

I work in mental health, what can PQ offer me?

PQ awards in mental health are set at higher specialist level. The Higher Specialist Award enables you to practice as an Approved Mental Health Practitioner under the Mental Health Act 1983 and a Best Interest Assessor in respect of Deprivation of Liberty Safeguards under the Mental Capacity Act 2005. Some employers make this a requirement of employment in mental health. So undertaking this award might not be your 'choice', but a requirement for employment. Advanced awards are also available and may allow you to go into very specialist areas of practice or research around mental health, however, it depends on what providers decide to offer. Check with local and national providers, for example, the Tavistock Centre (**www.tavi-port.org**), before you decide.

My role increasingly involves management responsibilities and/or I want to go into management – what can PQ offer me?

You may have options for PQ study at all three levels – specialist, higher specialist and advanced. However the leadership and management pathway is usually for managers who are already in post, so that you may find it hard to get on a programme unless you have supervisory responsibilities or are a senior practitioner. If you are a manager of a registered service, such as a residential home, your first priority will be obtaining an award that allows you to demonstrate competence against the Leadership and Management for Care Services National Occupational Standards. These recently replaced (September 2008) the Registered Manager Award. Once you have demonstrated competence against these new standards it should be possible for you to enter the leadership and management pathway through AP(E)L – the Accreditation of Prior (Experiential) Learning – processes.

I enjoy working with social work students, what can PQ offer me?

You may have options for study at a specialist or higher specialist award level. At the time of writing advanced awards in practice education have not been developed. At a specialist level you will achieve an understanding of how adults learn and the how you might assess a student's progress in the workplace. The Higher Specialist Award will provide much more depth and breadth in learning how to enable others within the workplace.

A number of research studies have evaluated the impact of PQ education on practitioner and employing organisation (Brown and Keen, 2004; Carpenter, 2005; Doel *et al.*, 2006, 2008; McCloskey, 2006) – those that do often take a snapshot or cross-sectional approach using questionnaires or interviews and use small sample sizes. This increasing body of evidence indicates that PQ education does have a positive and consistent impact on practice, but the level of impact very much depends on the individual and type of learning culture they are immersed in (Rushton and Martyn, 1990; Taylor, 1999; Cooper and Rixon, 2001; Mitchell, 2001; Postle *et al.*, 2002; Gauntlett, 2005; McCloskey, 2006; Ogilvie-Whyte, 2006; Doel *et al.*, 2008). Further research is needed to understand the impact PQ study has on social work practice and organisations – the type of impact Jane talks about in the case study below.

CASE STUDY 4.2

Jane's PQ story

I have thoroughly enjoyed the Specialist Award in Adult Social Work and feel that I have gained a great deal from it. I started the course three years after completing my Master's degree and Diploma in Social Work. I enrolled as I wished to continue my professional development and return to learning.

Colleagues have commented that my confidence has grown and I feel that my practice has improved. The course has provided a valuable opportunity to step back, analyse, reflect and consider my work and why we do what we do, which so easily becomes lost in a busy workplace. I now take a much more critical approach to government policies and agendas and have greater understanding of their likely impact upon local authorities, front-line workers and ultimately my role.

Some of the material covered on the course may be familiar to those who have recently qualified. However, the usefulness of revisiting this should not be overlooked. The views and beliefs that I held when I qualified have shifted and evolved as a result of spending several years actually 'doing' social work. Theories and material is looked at from a different and more critical stance that experience brings.

One of the most enjoyable aspects of the course was the chance to join with other practitioners away from the pressures of the work environment and share thoughts, feelings and frustrations of the job. This is a rare opportunity and I feel that I learnt a great deal through discussions with others.

I am currently completing the Enabling Work Based Learning module and am now supervising a final year student. Although the thought of being responsible for someone else's learning was initially a little daunting I am really enjoying the experience. Having a student is sharpening up my practice and knowledge and keeping me on my toes!

Anyone considering the Specialist Award needs to look beyond just the academic qualifi-cation. There is the potential to gain so much more from the course; you will grow as a practitioner, professional and possibly as an individual too. My skills base has expanded significantly which is not just going to benefit me but also my employer, be it current or prospective. Rather than just considering the Specialist Award in terms of its end result, see it as a journey where there is much to learn along the way

---

Before we move on to the topic of our final sub-section of this chapter – Post-Registration Training and Learning – we reproduce a useful checklist as shown in Box 4.1 from Doel *et al.*'s (2008) recent article in the journal *Social Work Education* – these questions are derived from survey and focus group findings and are best considered before starting PQ education. In the same article (Appendix 2) there are a series of questions for your employ ing agency and programme provider – do not be frightened to use them in supervision, via email or on the telephone to universities. Please also see Appendix 6 of this book for up to date tips from a PQ lecturer who has seen over 1700 students through the consolidation phase of the PQ framework.

ACTIVITY **4.6**

Consider Doel et al.'s questions in Box 4.1, Checklist for the PQ journey, on p 60. This is not intended to be a quick tick-box exercise, but an opportunity to spend some time with yourself (or someone whose opinion you value) to consider in some depth the questions that could make the difference between an enjoyable and successful PQ experience, and a burdensome chore that risks a wasted journey. It would be useful to write down your responses and to share them with the person who figures in your response to the third question (Doel et al., 2008, p 566).

Making PRTL real

The final part of this chapter is based on a presentation given at Community Care Live in London 2007 by Graham Ixer, Head of Social Work Education at the GSCC and looks at current PRTL (Post-Registration Training and Learning) policy and what it means in practice for registered social workers. Although not official guidance, what follows will be instruc-tive for newly qualified social workers wishing to renew their registration.

Social workers are, of course, required to renew their registration with the workforce regu-lator, the GSCC, every three years. In order to do this, you must show that you have completed a minimum of 90 hours or 15 days PRTL. Since compulsory registration has only been in place since 2005, the first cohort of social workers have only renewed their regis-tration in the past year and many more are coming up to renewal. It is therefore too early to draw firm conclusions about what people have been doing to meet this requirement. However, the GSCC is taking the opportunity to examine its policy around PRTL to look at

BOX 4.1

Checklist for the PQ journey

Does this post-qualifying study come at the right time for you?
Do you know what alternatives are available to you?

What (and who) is going to motivate you to carry on this journey if and when things get tough?
What do you hope success in your post-qualifying study will bring? What (and who) are going to help you enjoy this journey?

How do your colleagues view your post-qualifying study?
Is it important to you that they are supportive?

What will happen to your workload whilst you are studying?
Who do you need to talk to about this? What needs to happen to ensure that you have the time to ensure that your studies will be successful?

How will you make sure you 'have a life' during your studies?
What kind of support do you need from family and friends?

What aspects of your post-qualifying study do you fear might be disappointing/go wrong? What will you do about this if it happens?

Practicalities

Like all journeys it is important to make preparations and decide what to take with you.

- *Deadlines: as soon as you have deadlines for course work put them in your diary*

- *Study leave booked in your diary: work backwards from the deadlines to book study leave and, remember, these days must remain highest priority*

- *Course handbook: read through the course handbook carefully and make a note of questions that you want to ask and of whom*

- *Library membership: is library membership automatic or do you need to pursue it yourself?*

- *IT/computer support: what IT support do you need/can you expect? Do you need help to learn how to conduct electronic searches?*

Who is your agency contact person?
What will be the arrangements for contact and support?

Do you have regular access to someone who has done this, or a similar, journey before? If so, who is this? If not, is this going to be a significant void? If so, can you find someone? What role will your line manager play? Can you have sight of material that has been successful (e.g. a successful portfolio) – whilst recognising that the new systems will mean that there will be differences?

How will you know that the post-qualifying study has had an impact on your practice?

(Reproduced from Doel et al., 2008, pp 566–567 Appendix 1)

if and how we could be more prescriptive about the types of activity that can count towards a person's PRTL.

You may have a number of questions around PRTL. How do I interpret the requirements? What do I need to do to show that I have undertaken 15 days of further development and how much is enough? What constitutes relevant evidence of PRTL? The GSCC does not provide a prescriptive list of what should be submitted to prove PRTL. However, the following will provide indicative examples of what might be included and the parameters that help an individual to determine sufficiency and relevancy for their PRTL.

The diverse nature of the roles undertaken by social workers means that the types of PRTL undertaken by our registered workforce will be many and varied. As a modern regulator, the GSCC applies the principles of better regulation to all its work and activities and this includes its assessment of PRTL. The Better Regulation Executive says that all regulatory activity must be underpinned by the following principles:

- transparency;
- targeted;
- consistency:
- proportionate;
- accountable.

Each individual submission of PRTL from a registrant will be viewed by the GSCC with these principles in mind.

The GSCC does stipulate that PRTL should relate to the specific social work tasks associated with the social worker's current job. However, they are mindful that not all social workers will have a direct employer – some will be self-employed whilst others may not be involved in direct social work practice e.g. a social work lecturer or director of social services. This is why the requirements are written broadly to include a wide range of roles involved in delivering the social work task of better outcomes for those people who use services. Therefore, the examples which you can use to show how PRTL requirements have been met might include evidence of learning from a particular social work case study, project or task involved in your current role, although it does not have to be confined to this.

A key principle to consider is that undertaking PRTL should not be seen as a separate continuing professional development process but, where possible should integrate with existing processes. For most people their PRTL can be met easily through their routine performance appraisal process where they will set learning and development objectives. A record of this can be used as evidence of PRTL. Other people who do not have a formal performance management process at work may have to set something up specifically which records their PRTL. The GSCC provides a template for this as part of the pack given to all newly registered social workers. The weekly publication Community Care also provides a free on-line PRTL record template (available from **www. ccinform.co.uk/StaticPages/myPRTL.htm**).

The most important principle to bear in mind is to view PRTL as 'no big deal.' It is about recognising when learning has taken place and recording it on a regular basis so you do not forget. If you leave this until the end of your three-year registration period, then you might struggle to remember everything you have done. The following examples are meant to illustrate what types of learning experiences might be used for PRTL. This must not be seen as a *prescription* to follow or formal *guidance*, but merely something to help you think about the scope of learning and development activity that might be included. The relevance and sufficiency of any PRTL claim will be endorsed by your line manager, commissioner or other responsible person who can authenticate your PRTL. Undertaking PRTL in discussion with your endorser helps to ensure that PRTL is appropriate to your current role in social work.

What counts towards PRTL?

The GSCC does not stipulate in detail what a registered social worker needs to do to fulfil their PRTL requirements to enable flexibility, so all registrants can meet the requirements in different ways. This is in recognition of the broad range of roles and tasks undertaken by social workers. An efficient way to fulfil PRTL is through undertaking accredited learning because it can be verified easily. A completed PQ credit or full award is an excellent example of this.

However, non-accredited training may also be used, such as courses delivered in-house. For example, an in-house workshop on report writing that took place between 9–5 pm with an hour for lunch would constitute seven hours of training. However, after reflection the actual personal learning deriving from this might only equate to two to three hours of recorded PRTL. This is because it is unusual to undertake a course without already knowing something about the subject; therefore the learning may be substantial but will not reflect the total number of hours in attendance. However, this is not meant to provide a template for working out how many PRTL hours can be extrapolated from a learning experience, as this will be different for each person and their situation. In another situation the registrant may record all seven hours. *The key is to record the outcome of personal development and learning not the mere attendance.*

Other evidence which could be cited those new to the profession might include achievement of any of the new outcome statements newly qualified social workers (e.g. CWDC, 2008). All newly qualified social workers will have a set of standards that they must achieve during their first year in practice and could record this outcome as part of their PRTL. Most of this activity will be consolidating their qualifying training.

The following are indicative of what might be used as legitimate evidence towards PRTL requirements:

- outcomes of supervision discussions;
- appraisal activities;
- learning and development outcomes from a case conference;
- learning from work that went wrong – discussions with line manager about mistakes made and rectified;
- undertaking a new task;

- secondment to a new department or role;

- taking a family to panel (fostering) for the first time and discussing the learning with their manager;

- implementing a new assessment system after training;

- reading a Social Care Institute for Excellence (SCIE) practice article and relating it to their own experience;

- reading a book on social work practice;

- reading an article that relates to an issue or problem that is currently being tackled in their practice;

- writing an article or book on social work;

- teaching social work;

- undertaking research in social work;

- managing resources, people, systems for the first time that contribute to social work practice;

- developing social work policy and learning how it changes practice;

- practice teaching a student for the first time;

- putting into practice a new idea, policy or practice change.

Two fictitious examples of how social workers have met the PRTL requirements follow.

BOX **4.2**

Example of a registrant practising social work in children's services

John works in an intake and assessment team for children and families. As part of his Post-Registration, Training and Learning, he undertook a number of one day training courses in safeguarding which amounted to a total of five days. He also included the learning outcome from a number of difficult child protection case conferences. As a consequence of supervision and case conferences he was able to reflect on his own involvement and with the aid of hindsight allocate a number of hours specifically related to his learning from these cases. This totalled 21 hours or three days of PRTL.

John also included learning from a number of in house workshops which amounted to two days. A new computer system had been installed in his authority and he used his learning of the system to reflect up to three days of PRTL. John also included evidence from his appraisal, in particular discussions with his manager about how he had developed greater confidence in dealing with aggressive parents. He found the potential violence something difficult to manage and after many discussions and trying out new approaches he was able to intervene more successfully and with confidence. He recorded three days for this.

BOX **4 . 3**

Example of a social work manager

Leona has just implemented a new staffing structure which has taken nearly six months to plan and implement and has taken most of her time and energy. Her new team is now in place and since then she has spent time talking to her new staff, her manager and customers and reflected upon the experience. Given the task again she would have done things differently. She recorded eight days PRTL to reflect the outcome of her learning from this task.

She took on the job of mentoring a colleague over a year and complemented this with personal reading on the subject. As this was the first time she had ever mentored someone, she felt she had gained substantial learning from the experience and recorded five days. She had also completed the last part of her MSc degree in forensic social work which had taken her five years to complete. She recorded 30 days of learning for the period she was registered.

Leona also recorded learning acquired from a very difficult experience. She had to discipline a member of staff which finally resulted in the staff member being dismissed. Although she had HR support she felt she had to manage this on her own. She spent a lot of time with her supervisor discussing the issues and felt that she had learnt a great deal and recorded three days of PRTL.

These two examples demonstrate that if the learning leads to developmental change in a registrant then it is likely to be relevant. Early evidence shows that most registrants record above the 15 days minimum required. It is therefore quite easy to meet this minimum standard as most social workers are required within their normal job role to undertake development or training of some sort or another. It is important for you to start to record your PRTL as soon as possible. Every experience and action yields potential learning and therefore potential PRTL. It would be good practice for you to discuss your PRTL outcomes with your manager on a regular basis. The GSCC's (2004) Code of Practice for Social Care Workers underpins your personal learning and development and this is backed up by the code for employers who must ensure that you are supported in meeting registration requirements. To stay on the register all registrants must ensure they remain competent in their role (GSCC, 2005b). PRTL is the test to make this a reality.

Summary of key points

- The ability to continually learn, develop and adapt are key skills that newly qualified social workers need to embrace.

- Each of the levels of the PQ framework (specialist, higher specialist and advanced) corresponds to different stages of professional development. As a newly qualified social worker you are most likely to enter the framework at specialist level.

- PRTL should not be seen as a separate continuing professional development process but, where possible should integrate with and enhance existing processes. Remember to record all appropriate informal and formal learning activities.

Brown, K and Rutter, L (2008) *critical thinking for social work.* 2nd edn. Exeter: Learning Matters.

Practical, down to earth guidance in an easily digestible format.

Community Care Magazine's PTRL zone – available from: **www.ccinform.co.uk/StaticPages/myPRTL.htm** (accessed 28 August 2008)

Community Care provide useful guidance on PRTL here.

Chapter 5

Managing the personal: from surviving to thriving in social work

Kate Howe, Mike Henry and Kay Renshaw
with a contribution from Jonathan Parker

This chapter will help you to meet the following National Occupational Standards for Social Work.

- Key role 5: manage and be accountable with supervision and support for your own social work practice within your organisation, unit 14: manage and be accountable for your own work

- Key role 6: demonstrate professional competence in social work practice, unit 19 work within agreed standards of social work practice and ensure your own professional development, unit 20: manage complex ethical issues, dilemmas and conflicts.

Introduction

As a newly qualified social worker you may already be aware of the effect social work practice can have on the individual. You may have experienced some feelings of stress, or witnessed colleagues reacting to stressful situations. Social work is no ordinary job as professionals engage with individuals with varying wants, needs, and demands. Couple to this, a working environment where frequent changes in policies and practices abound and it is to be expected that social work practice is, at times, stressful (Collins, 2008). However, stress does not always have to lead to negative outcomes and can indeed lead to positive outcomes if managed appropriately (Collins, 2008).

Managing stress is, of course, just one aspect of managing yourself and the transition from student to professional. In interviews (carried out by two of the authors Mike Henry and Kay Renshaw) asking 18 newly qualified childcare social workers about their journey into the world of social work many highlight the emotional core at the centre of this transition. They speak of experiencing a big difference between the rhetoric and reality of practice. High expectations often became disappointments. Using words such as *'I felt out of my depth'* and *'I felt I was thrown into the work which really affected me as a person'* these workers emphasise their emotional journeys. They talk of *losing their confidence,* feeling *de-skilled, anxious and scared.* And while these might be considered normal reactions to a transformational process, evidence suggests that if these feelings continue over a long period of time, they result in serious consequences, for example, deep-seated feelings of dissatisfaction and emotional exhaustion (Stanley *et al.*, 2008).

Therefore, the main tenets of this chapter are around identifying, understanding, and developing strategies to combat these types of feeling and supporting the emotional core that is central to maintaining your personal health and high standards of professional practice. Being aware of your emotions is a crucial part of this process as is the ability to manage them in order to develop professionally and address some of the opportunities we laid out for you in Chapter 4. Our view is that by looking after yourself and by managing your professional environment you will be more able to work effectively with people who use services and carers – one of the key factors that motivates social workers to stay in the profession (Cameron, 2003; Huxley *et al.*, 2005). Whilst the second part of this chapter considers strategies to develop your emotional core, the first part focuses on the personal issues you are likely to have to manage as a newly qualified social worker. First, we consider how the personal 'you' interacts with the professional 'you'.

Managing the personal in social work

It is easy to think that the qualified social worker has learnt to distance themselves from any personal 'feelings' and is therefore 'objective' even in the most difficult of situations. However, the idea that your own beliefs and emotions can be completely hidden in any professional relationship is flawed; they will always leak out in some way. It is much more effective to acknowledge them. This can then create a balance between professional behaviour and personal thoughts and feelings which is crucial to good social work and good health.

Harrison and Ruch (2007) distinguish between 'self-less' social work where the emphasis is on the *doing* of the tasks, and 'self-ish' social work that has self-knowledge and awareness at the heart of *being* a social worker. By rejecting the description of 'self-less', they challenge the traditional social work perspective of a distant, neutral, and emotionless professional as lacking true focus on people who use services. To practise from a 'self-ish' perspective forces us to consider and understand the interpersonal dynamics of an interaction. Personal self-awareness as well as knowledge of others is at least as important as knowing 'what to do' and 'how to do it'. Developing this understanding leads to an appreciation of the unique relationship between yourself, the people who use services as individuals, and the social context, and thereby a true personalised service. To attempt to reduce this understanding to standardised and rational behaviour patterns loses the depth and heart of the social work relationship.

ACTIVITY **5.1**

What are some of the differences for you in your current role between 'doing' social work and 'being' a social worker?

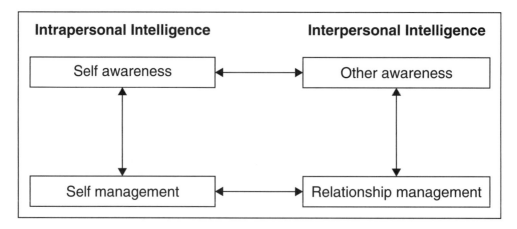

Figure 5.1 The concept of emotional intelligence

Emotional intelligence

The concept of emotional intelligence, popularised by Goleman (1996), helps gain insight into *being* a social worker. It is also a useful model to help underpin the development of unique and positive relationships. Morrison (2007, p 251) portrays the basic model as having four domains as represented in Figure 5.1.

As the arrows indicate all the domains in Figure 5.1 are related. Understanding this 'inter-relatedness' is key to you being able to work in stressful and emotionally charged situations. As Shulman (1999, cited in Morrison 2007, p 251) points out, a social worker can only really understand and be in touch with the feelings of those he or she works with if they have the ability to acknowledge their own emotions – in other words, to be self-aware.

Self-awareness

Goleman (1996, p 46) defines self-awareness as the *sense of an ongoing attention to one's internal states*. As we have already stated, to be effective a newly qualified social worker must realise the impact of self in the professional social work task. Practitioners are emotional beings as much as people who use services. You may think it easy to recognise your emotions when faced with an angry user of services, but do you have the same level of awareness when completing the same care assessment paperwork for the hundredth time? Are you filling in a form or really listening to what your client is saying? It is all too easy lose this focus – so finding a way to notice the link between emotional triggers, any subsequent feelings and/or effect on your behaviour and performance, is important. Honest feedback from trusted colleagues can be a good way to gain new perspectives on your emotional well-being.

Self-management

Self-management operates at two interrelated levels, the emotional and practical. Both have a role to play in enabling you to manage in the practice environment.

Emotional

Good self-management is about displaying an appropriate emotional response that is proportionate to the situation you are facing. Strong emotions are, of course, the source of much energy and creativity. Anger can be a great source of motivation, so as an emotionally intelligent social worker you will have a range of different ways working with positive and negative emotions (Held, 2009). Good emotional self-management means developing choice about how, when and where feelings are expressed. It is most definitely unhealthy to suppress or stifle your emotions and this can lead to stressful reactions that are physically unhealthy (e.g. raised blood pressure) and can impair your thinking and social interactions.

Practical

Good self-management at a practical level can enhance your emotional response, allowing you time and space to develop appropriate reactions to stressful situations. Practical self-management strategies include the following.

- Supervision – arranging regular supervision sessions, attending sessions prepared with the issues you wish to discuss, including emotional issues. Collins (2008, p 1182) argues research suggests . . . *regular, extensive supervision, better informed and more sensitive supervision is likely to provide more effective support for social workers*. If you have not done so already, please refer to Chapter 3 – the last part of the chapter centres on supervision.

- Support from colleagues – research in the UK highlights the importance to practitioners of developing support systems from colleagues, for example mentors and/or 'buddy systems' (Collins, 2008). Chapter 6 focuses on joining and contributing to a team and should also be helpful in this regard.

- Managing your diary and allowing time to complete tasks – is arranging a visit immediately after a particularly difficult multi-disciplinary strategy meeting really the best time? Could this visit be undertaken at a different time thereby giving you time to address any practical or emotional issues that may arise from the meeting? While there are frequently deadlines to work to, ask yourself the question; are these imposed on me at an organisational level or am I putting pressure on myself?

- Take regular breaks – take any breaks you are entitled to during the working day, even if it is just ten minutes. Ensure you take regular leave with time for yourself and/or with your family; not to catch up on work.

- Prioritise and be realistic – social work practitioners can have an overdeveloped sense of responsibility, leading to the setting of unrealistic goals. Also, be clear about what *must* be done now and what can be left until later.

Stress and burnout

Stress is simply how the individual responds, at a physical and emotional level, to the demands of the job. Collins (2008, p 1176) provides further clarity on the nature of stress when he states:

> Stress has been said to arise from the disparity between the 'perceived' demands made on the individual and their 'perceived' ability to cope with these demands suggesting that *if demands are high and perceived ability to cope are high, then a person will not feel stressed.*

This suggests stress associated with social work practice does not inevitably lead to negative experiences. Furthermore, Collins (2008, p 1188) suggests that individuals require an awareness of themselves, their strengths and weaknesses, along with *knowledge and understanding of the important components of stress, job satisfaction, coping, hardiness, resilience and control* – all of which can be part of solutions, as the second part of the chapter points out.

The working life of a social worker, as we highlighted in the introduction, can be very stressful indeed. All potentially stressful situations can result in a condition often talked about in social work called 'burnout'. This can involve feelings of:

- frustration, helplessness and powerlessness in the working environment;
- having the emotional energy sucked out of you;
- being fenced in and unable to escape;
- demoralisation;
- irritation;
- cynicism about your job and any possibility of success;
- overwhelming tiredness;
- wanting to indulge in escapist behaviours as a way of freeing yourself from your work situation.

(Tickle, 2007, pp 37–39)

These are really crucial signs of exhaustion, stress and burnout. It is vital to seek support from a supervisor or colleague if you identify with these feelings. Prevention is the key to creating and maintaining a work environment which minimises stress, and good supervision can be a major factor in the prevention of burnout.

From surviving to thriving

There are also other strategies of good emotional self-management that can diminish feelings of stress. Collins (2007) defines the concept of emotional resilience as your general ability to develop flexible and resourceful strategies to external and internal stressors. This idea is similar to Kobasa's (1979, cited in Kamya, 2000) model of 'hardiness' which is based on evaluating someone's ability to handle and manage problems or difficulties and consists of the characteristics of challenge, commitment and control.

- If you relish challenges you will seek out opportunities for continual growth and learning, rather than routine, security and staying within your comfort zones.

- If you have a strong value base and are committed to your work you will find ways to see the positive in situations.

- A strong sense of control will enable you to believe you can influence the course of events around you, rather than being a victim of circumstance.

Kamya (2000) highlights that younger social workers tend to have lower levels of 'hardiness' and fewer coping strategies, and therefore may be more prone to stress and burnout. This is why it is important to positively develop coping and management strategies which address the issues of workload, emotional stress and conflict.

Maddi's 'hardiness training' (1998) has a number of suggestions that you could usefully adapt to your own working life.

- *Techniques of situational reconstruction.* This involves seeking a broader understanding of a situation. Using reflection skills and models developed during your qualifying degree programme are good examples of this. Taking time on your own, or with a team colleague or in supervision, to 'unpack' a difficult interaction can bring clarity and emotional resolution.

- *Focusing.* This is based on Gendlin's work (1996) and entails developing a body related understanding of a situation. Being aware of where you are holding tension in your body is an example of this. A way of doing this could be to take some time out on your own – ten minutes should be enough. Note where your body is tense and where you feel comfortable. Breathing and stretching exercises can help unblock those areas that are tense.

- *Compensatory self-improvement.* This means accepting unchangeable situations without bitterness or self pity – see the following section on areas of acceptance, influence and control.

Developing your own resilience in the ways described above can help prevent you from feeling overwhelmed by work and view the challenges of social work as opportunities.

ACTIVITY 5.2

Think of a situation when you have been in a high emotional state and have managed your feelings positively. Remember specifically:

- *What were you doing?*
- *What did you say?*
- *How did you feel?*
- *What actions did you take?*
- *What enabled you to do this?*
  - o *relating to the environment;*
  - o *relating to yourself and what beliefs were you holding about yourself?*
- *What was the result?*

Knowing the answers to these simple questions can give you a specific awareness of what you do well and enable you to repeat those strategies in other situations.

Anchoring

Another approach that may help develop positive self-management when faced with difficult situations is called 'anchoring'. This can be useful when giving evidence in court, or presenting a report at a case conference, or when you know you have a difficult interview to do. An anchor is a stimulus that becomes a trigger to make us respond in a certain way. It can be visual, auditory, a feeling, a smell, or a taste. Existing anchors can set off emotions by remembering a particular experience. For example, hearing the first three notes of your favourite piece of music can create a warm feeling inside as you remember not only the rest of the music, but also any associated memories. A picture of your family by your desk can evoke a sense of joy. Equally, anchors can be negative. Certain places, people, events can make us feel upset, sad, or afraid. For instance, just the smell of perfume worn by a critical teacher can bring back negative memories. You may be unaware of many of these anchors – in other words, they operate at a sub-conscious level. We can use positive anchors to improve our ability to work in difficult circumstances, exercise more control over our behaviour and actions, and achieve outcomes we are working towards. Try the following activity.

ACTIVITY **5.3**

Anchoring

Find a quiet space where you will not be interrupted. You may need a pen and a blank piece of paper. Allow about ten minutes.

- *Step 1: think about the situation you are preparing for and decide on the 'state' you want to be in. For example, you may write down 'confident' or 'assertive', but be specific about what sort of 'confident' or 'assertive' you mean. Add more precise words, so that you have a really comprehensive understanding.*

- *Step 2: decide on the 'anchor' that you want to use. This needs to be easy to apply in the situation you want to use it and has to be distinct, in your control, short and easily repeatable. It can be visual, auditory or kinaesthetic. Hand gestures may work well, such as clenching your fist, pressing your first finger and thumb together, or pulling your earlobe. Visual or auditory ones can include looking at a picture or a repeating a particular word.*

- *Step 3: think of a specific occasion when you remember being in the positive state you wrote down in Step 1. It must be a positive memory and you need to be central. Then spend a minute remembering more about the situation. For example, think about the people who are also there and their movements and expressions; remember any colours, voices or other sounds. What were you doing, saying and thinking – were you walking around or sitting down, talking or listening, what were you saying to yourself?*

- *Step 4: then, when the memory is really strong – repeat the anchor you decided upon in Step 2, and hold it for a count of five. Let go and relax as your memory and feelings created in Step 3 start to diminish.*

ACTIVITY **5.3** *(CONT.)*

- Step 5: then let go of that memory completely by doing something totally different for 20 seconds. Stand up, turn around and sit down again, look around the room or remember what you ate at your last meal.

- Step 6: repeat Step 3, 4 and 5 a couple of times to strengthen the anchor – and this can be repeated regularly to reinforce the feelings. Then 'fire' the anchor on its own and notice how your state changes to the one you identified in Step 1. Some people find it helpful to close their eyes.

- Now think about the situation from Step 1; imagine it is happening and use your anchor. Using your imagination and noticing what is happening will aid preparation substantially.

You can use this and other anchors to recall positive memories and create a positive emotional state. You will find that the more you build these anchors, the more you will be in control of your actions and feel positively able to achieve your goals.

(Adapted from Henwood and Lister 2007, p 159)

CASE STUDY **5.2**

Anchoring – an editor's tale

One of the editors (Jonathan Parker) remembers his first time giving evidence in court as a qualified social worker. Having observed court proceedings on a number of occasions and having taken and supported people at court hearings, the process and environment was well known. However, when it came to being responsible for giving evidence and ensuring the best outcome for those involved it was a nerve-wracking experience. It was important to remain anchored to the reasons for being in court and to the planned approach determined beforehand. He had with him two well-worn pebbles that he held and moved around in his hand which allowed him to focus, take time, relax and concentrate on the task.

You may recognise that these simple autogenic and 'self-talk' techniques derive from neurolinguistic programming (O'Connor, 2006; Henwood and Lister, 2007) and cognitive behavioural approaches. They can help you in your social worker role as well as being a process you may share with someone who uses services.

Areas of concern, influence and control

A further aspect of self-management is having an awareness of where our attention is. Covey (1989) distinguishes between areas of concern and areas of influence. Within our area of concern are all the topics that we spend time and energy on; ranging from health, family, climate change, organisational structure, how much we are being paid, and so on.

However, many of these subjects are outside of our influence and control. It can be tempting to focus our energy (particularly our mental energy in the form of worry, frustration, irritation and complaining) on those things in life that most concern us. But if we have no influence over them that energy can be said to be wasted. By focusing your effort on what you are able to influence, you are likely to be more effective in your interventions and thereby increase your capacity for influence. Covey (1989) characterises those who focus on areas of influence and control as proactive and those who focus on what is beyond their control as reactive. People who are more reactive are more likely to feel a victim of circumstance and blame others for problems. Proactive people are more likely to be able to widen their influence as they focus on areas they can change or control.

Charles and Butler (2004) offer a framework of control, influence and acceptance which extends Covey's model in a way that is relevant to social work. It focuses on managing the tension between the ideals of social work (that as a newly qualified social worker are fresh in your memory) and the practice realities that often cause stress and dissatisfaction. As a newly qualified social worker, it is worth considering Charles and Butler's (2004) distinctions (Table 5.1) between situations where you have control, those where you have some influence, and those where you have neither of these and need to reach a state of acceptance. Focusing your energy on productive areas is likely to decrease stress levels and bring job satisfaction.

ACTIVITY 5.4

Table 5.1 takes different aspects of your role at work and suggests which tasks are in the categories of control, influence and accept. Take a few minutes to consider how much control and influence you have in your work. Do you agree with the contents of the table? What else might you add to these columns? Then consider whether the statements in the accept column are accurate for you? What might you add or alter? How do these distinctions change your view of your work? (Adapted from Charles and Butler, 2004).

So far we have considered the role of the personal and a range of intrapersonal activities that can help us acknowledge and manage our emotions in practice. We now turn to awareness of others and the management of relationships.

Awareness of others and the management of relationships

Good social work is conducted through effective relationships (Ruch, 2005) with anti-oppressive practice at its heart. Morrison (2007) believes that interpersonal intelligence is central to high quality practice (see Figure 5.1). Throughout your qualifying education there will have been an emphasis on building communication and relationship skills. However, one area of relationship management that can cause much disquiet and anxiety for newly qualified social workers is working with conflict (Brown *et al.*, 2007). Conflict is an inevitable part of life arising from differences in needs, values and interests and is a state of discord or disharmony. What is important is how we respond to and manage it. We can respond constructively or destructively – often when we respond constructively we do not realise we have done so. When we view conflict in organisations or teams as positive it can:

Table 5.1 Control, influence and accept

	Control	Influence	Accept
Personal	• Allocation of time • Use of skills • Relationship building • Values	• Team development • Express appropriate dissatisfaction about agency policies	• Appreciation of own strengths and limitations • Preferred methods of working
Professional	• Selection of working methods • Development of own expertise/specialisms	• Using professional credibility and research to influence other professionals	• Uncertainty • What is possible to achieve and what is not • That small scale changes can transform lives
Organisational	• Skills in work/systems management • Your image at work of organised, professional worker	• Collective action; participation in lobbying/union groups	• Agency limitations • Benefits of work (e.g. plan holidays and take time of in lieu)

Adapted from Charles and Butler (2004)

- highlight underlying issues;

- motivate to deal with underlying problems;

- enhance a mutual understanding;

- stimulate a sense of urgency;

- discourage avoidance of problems;

- sharpen understanding of issues and goals.

However, when conflict is responded to destructively, it can take a tremendous amount of our energy and attention. We can resort to unhelpful strategies because of our emotional reactions.

ACTIVITY **5.5**

Pause for thought: Think of a time when you responded positively in a situation of conflict and note these down.

- *What did you do?*

- *How did you respond?*

- *What were you thinking or feeling at the time?*

The thoughts and skills you demonstrated may then help you next time you are in a situation of conflict. Now compare your response with the following model of conflict resolution. Thomas and Ruble's (1976, cited in Huczinski and Buchanan, 2007) model of conflict resolution (Figure 5.2) is based on:

- how assertive or unassertive each party is in pursuing their own concerns;

- how co-operative or not each party is in meeting the needs of the other.

They distinguish five approaches to resolving conflict, ranging from avoidance to collaboration as displayed in Table 5.3.

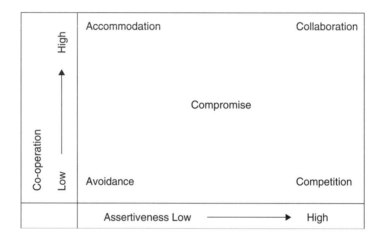

Figure 5.2 Thomas and Ruble's (1976) model of conflict resolution (cited in Huczinski and Buchanan 2007, p 777)

ACTIVITY 5.6

Clearly the most useful approach is collaboration and there are many reasons why this may not be the approach always used. Study Table 5.3. It is worth spending a few minutes considering different situations of conflict you have encountered and recognise the factors that led to particular outcomes.

To end this chapter we present a four step model that you can use to help you find collaborative resolutions to conflict.

A four step model to resolve conflict

This model is adapted from Ross (2004) and Dilts and DeLozier (2000).

Table 5.3 Details of the approaches of conflict resolution

Approach	Behaviour	Thoughts	Likely outcome
Avoidance	Ignore it and hope it will go away! Pretend it hasn't happened. Withdraw from any situations where conflict might happen.	Feel inadequate and helpless. Believe that conflict is harmful.	Frustration, because the conflict remains unresolved.
Competition	Shouting; refusing to listen to others. Manipulating others to your way of thinking. Using power games to force submission.	It is important to get the right solution. Others are to blame for this. Hurt feelings are unavoidable.	Conflict is resolved at a superficial level, but there is long term damage to relationships as one party feels defeated and possibly humiliated.
Accommodation	Give way. Make sure the other person is not upset. Maintain the peace at any cost.	My views are not important. Amicable relationships are the top priority.	Conflict is resolved through submission and compliance and alternative views not being considered.
Compromise	Search for a quick solution to move on as fast as possible. Get to an agreement that both can 'live with'.	Conflict drains energy that can be better used elsewhere. It needs to be resolved quickly to prevent bad feelings.	A 'quick and dirty' solution is found, which can work. A better answer could have been produced given more time.
Collaboration	Time is spent listening to each other and discussion focuses on understanding all sides of the problem and looking for integrative solutions.	There is a way to solve this problem. It is not about winning. It is about respecting the other person – even if we disagree with them. It is important to spend time finding a creative solution.	Conflict is resolved through a solution to the problem that all parties are committed to. All involved feel the process has been fair.

Adapted from Whetton *et al.*, 2000, cited in Huczinski and Buchanan, 2007

Step 1: in preparation

- Accept the following two statements about the other person.

  o That their behaviour is the best way they know of acting in the current context.

  o That their behaviour has a positive (although sometimes unconscious) intention

- *(Remembering these statements during the negotiation will demonstrate a deep respect for that person)*

- Ask yourself the following questions about the other person.

  o What are the circumstances that are making them behave in this way?

  o What is motivating them to behave like this?

  o How do the answers to these questions help explain the person's behaviour?

- Think about why your position is important to you.

- Decide on a possible outcome that you are prepared to modify during discussion.

- Be determined to find a good, collaborative solution and be prepared to spend time in that process.

Step 2: in discussion

- Be able to manage and express your emotions and views positively. Recognise when it will be useful to express your emotions. Techniques such as deep breathing, sitting back, taking time out, looking up at the ceiling for a count of five are sometimes useful here.

- It is important that you say what you need to say – in a way that can be heard by the other person.

- Listen to the other point of view and validate their contributions.

- Find out what is important to them about their position and remember your own perspective. Consider whether there is any consensus. Any consensus will usually be at a higher level than the area of disagreement. For example, if you disagree about how many team meetings to hold in a month, then work out what you agree about the function of the meetings. This can develop a new understanding of the issue. Take care to stay focused on this issue.

- From this consensus position, you can now work on finding other solutions or alternatives to achieve a shared position. Identify a number of alternatives before deciding on which one is best. These may be a combination of your original positions; though it may be helpful to identify one that is distinct from them.

- Decide on which choice or combination of choices is going to be most effective and workable.

Step 3: resolving the conflict, even if there is no solution

If the conflict is not resolved in discussion, consider the following strategies.

- Time out – agree to disagree for the present time and plan to meet again later (it is often surprising how much can change during any interval).

- Mediation – use someone you both trust as neutral and impartial. Going to mediation is not failure – it is a courageous step that recognises it is important to find a resolution.

Step 4: looking after yourself

Resolving conflict is hard work whether you reach a resolution or not. If the conflict remains unresolved ensure you spend some time letting go of your emotions about the issue – try physical exercise, or a relaxation exercise, or talk it through with a *neutral* friend. For a comprehensive relaxation routine and other useful tips look at the *Stress Self Help Guide* by Maunder and Cameron (2006).

Summary of key points

- At the heart of social work is the 'personal'. Good practice is dependent on growing and valuing this perspective in all of the unique relationships you create.

- Thriving in social work involves development of your emotional intelligence which means paying attention to your intrapersonal intelligence and your interpersonal intelligence. This, as part of your continuing professional development, takes time and conscious effort. Reflection will assist your progress.

- Stress is part of the job – being aware of it can help to overcome it.

- It is up to you to manage yourself – no-one else will – so give some thought to how you look after yourself, when you reward yourself and how you recognise and celebrate your achievements.

FURTHER READING

Conflict resolution network – go to **www.crnhq.org/index.php**.

This website is a great resource for those considering any aspects of conflict resolution. It has a huge variety of downloadable free materials and an easily accessible self-study guide, which encourages you to develop confidence in conflict situations.

Henwood S and Lister, J (2007) *NLP and coaching for healthcare professionals.* Chichester: Wiley.

Although this book has originally been written for 'healthcare professionals' it is equally relevant to social workers. It is a self-help book that offers many tools and exercises designed to increase your self-awareness and self-confidence.

Howe, D (2008) *The emotionally intelligent social worker.* Basingstoke: Palgrave.

This book provides a readable and in-depth analysis of emotional intelligence and its uses in social work. Much of the focus and examples are related to social work practice and there is a helpful final chapter which considers the practitioner perspective and working under stress.

Chapter 6

Joining and contributing to a team

Anne Quinney with contributions from George (carer), Liz Slinn (NQSW), Marion Davis (Strategic Director of Children's Services) and Ivan Gray

This chapter will enable you to prepare for the following National Occupational Standards for Social Work.

- Key Role 5: manage and be accountable, with supervision and support, for your own social work practice within your organisation.

  o Work with multi-disciplinary and multi-organisational teams, networks and systems.

  o Contribute to evaluating the effectiveness of the team, network or system.

  o Deal constructively with disagreements and conflict within relationships.

- Key Role 6: demonstrate professional competence in social work practice.

  o Work within agreed standards of social work practice and ensure own professional development.

  o Manage complex ethical issues, dilemmas and conflicts.

  o Contribute to the promotion of best social work practice.

Introduction

As a newly qualified social worker you will be joining a team in one of the many settings in which social work is practised. In this chapter, you are going to consider a range of topics that will help you to feel prepared for your new role as a newly qualified social worker, including:

- what you bring to the team as a newly qualified social worker; and

- what you need to know to help you work effectively in a team.

In this chapter you will also meet Liz, a newly qualified social worker working in a children and families team and hear in her own words about her experiences of joining a team; and Marion, a Strategic Director of Children's Services.

But what do we mean by a 'team'?

Jelphs and Dickinson (2008, p 8) offer a definition by Morhman *et al*. (1995, p 4) which describes a team as:

a group of individuals who work together to produce products or deliver services for which they are held mutually accountable. Team members share goals and are mutually held accountable for meeting them, they are interdependent in their accomplishment, and they affect the results through interactions with one another. Because the team is held collectively accountable, the work of interaction with one another is included among the responsibilities of each member.

The emphasis on shared purpose and interdependence is important. In this chapter, we will be looking at the things you can do to prepare for and enhance your contribution to the organisation and the team.

It is highly likely that you will be working with people from other professional backgrounds. As stated in the social work subject benchmarks (Quality Assurance Agency [QAA], 2008, para 3.7):

social work increasingly takes place in an inter-agency context, and social workers work collaboratively with others towards interdisciplinary and cross-professional objectives.

A statement from the Climbié Report (Laming, 2003 para 17.112) highlights the importance of working closely with people from other professional groups and agencies:

It is clear that the safeguarding of children will continue to depend upon services such as health, education, housing, police and social services working together.

When teams work well this can impact on the satisfaction of people who access care services and their carers. Research undertaken by Borrill *et al.* (2003) and Brown *et al.* (2003) indicates that good team working involving participation, support for innovation, reflexivity, and support from team members can impact positively on the satisfaction of people who use services. So what can you do to contribute to good team working?

CASE STUDY **6.1**

What do I bring to the team as a newly qualified social worker?

Liz, a newly qualified social worker, describes some of the important qualities that a newly qualified social worker brings to a team:

- *fresh enthusiasm and energy;*

- *a head bursting with lots of theories but wanting to put them into practice;*

- *high standards and expectations of yourself and other professionals;*

- *hopes and aspirations for people who use services and carers;.*

- *a willingness to share ideas and new research;*

- *different ways of approaching work;*

- *a willingness to learn and absorb as much information as possible;*

- *a willingness to challenge practice, thinking and attitudes;*

- *up-to-date IT skills;*

- *a range of knowledge and skills gained from working with other agencies on placement.*

Liz clearly captures the qualities of openness to new situations, the capacity for contributing new ideas and a readiness to learn and develop. These can all make a very positive contribution to your new team, but you will need to be careful at first that you do not frighten people off. Your team will already have established relationships and ways of working so you will need to gradually gain peoples' trust and find a place for yourself. So how do you build the trust that is perhaps the foundation of an effective team?

Developing trust

Trust is an important dimension of working collaboratively, described by Stapleton (1998, p 12) as an 'essential attribute' which depends on the 'support, honesty and integrity' of all concerned. Trust is also embedded in the values statement that underpins the National Occupational Standards for Social Work (Topss England, 2002). So what does trust involve and how might you as a newly qualified social worker develop this quality? Thomas *et al.* (2009a), building on the work of Stapleton (1998) and Lawson (2004) tell us that trust involves:

- valuing other people;
- building relationships based on mutual respect;
- explicitly acknowledging each person's unique contribution;
- being explicit about policies that you have to work within;
- seeking to understand the constraints on another person;
- being honest and realistic about what you can do.

And that the following behaviours are likely to break or undermine trust:

- not doing what you have agreed;
- 'free riding' or leaving other people to do the work;
- offering more than you can deliver;
- alluding to policies in a vague way to give excuses for taking action;
- moaning about another professional;
- exploiting the difficulties of others in order to show yourself in a more positive light;
- working on the assumption that unresolved difficulties encountered in previous contacts will re-emerge.

In building trust in your team it is also worth bearing in mind that socialising is important as it allows people to get to know each other properly. A team chatting over coffee or a team lunch is not time wasted.

ACTIVITY 6.1

Set some regular time aside to reflect on the strategies that you are using to develop and sustain trust in working relationships with colleagues and with carers and people who use services. Try to ensure that you are developing helpful rather than hindering strategies.

Beyond trusting relationships what are the other factors that can contribute to good team working? It is a good idea at this point to remind yourself of the group work theory that you may have studied as part of your qualifying training. The concepts that underpin our understanding of groups can all be applied to team working. So, for instance, you may well remember the stages of group development, forming, storming, norming, and performing? Like groups, teams are seen to go through a number of distinct stages from the point of formation until their termination. Each stage is part of a progression that leads towards increasingly better performance (Tuckman, 1965). As a team member you will be seeking to help develop your team so that it develops and becomes more effective, improving its performance over time.

Developing team effectiveness
What are the advantages of effective team working?
You will be able to have an impact in your day to day work in improving the way in which the team works. In Figure 6.1 you can see that improved team working can have an impact on the satisfaction of people working in the organisation and on the outcomes for people who use services and carers and on their satisfaction with the service. In turn, these can influence the performance of the organisation and generate further positive outcomes.

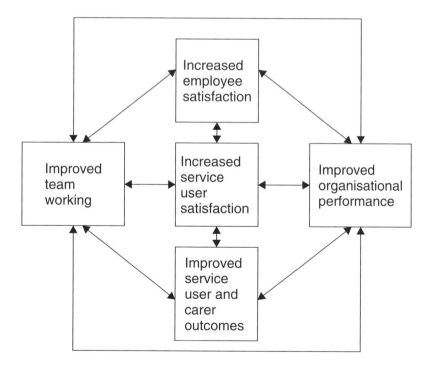

Figure 6.1 The impact of improved team working

(Adapted from Jelphs and Dickinson, 2008, p 16)

ACTIVITY 6.2

Spend a few moments considering what you know about group process dynamics and its place in social work and social care. Note the similarities to team development and consider how you might use your learning to understand your place within the team and the potential contribution you can make to its development.

Use the team development audit tool in Table 6.1 to structure and document your reflections on your team, informed by your understanding of group work skills and group dynamics.

Auditing team effectiveness

Some other useful questions for you to consider are:

- could the team be seen in anyway to be 'stuck' in unhelpful behaviours?
- what might I do to help them move on?
- is there a team development plan that has been discussed and agreed with the team?

Team meetings

Teams often hold formal meetings in order to share information, plan, problem-solve, and learn. Most of us interact with our teams on a daily basis outside of these meetings, but sometimes if a team is dispersed and people work very independently it can be the only time you can get together. In either case team meetings can be important events. They can make a big contribution to how effectively a team carries out its tasks and how good its relationships are. You may find it useful to reflect on your role in the team, and to consider your contribution in team meetings. Try using this checklist to help you reflect on your contribution to team meetings.

How do I behave in team meetings?

- Am I happy with my contribution to the team so far?
- Do I help others to express their ideas?
- Do I listen well?
- Do I communicate my ideas well?
- Do I avoid conflict when I shouldn't?
- Do I tend to hold on to my own opinions without taking account of the views of other?
- Do I take on a leadership role?
- Am I too quiet?
- Do I give in too quickly when challenged?
- Do I tend to stick to my own views despite criticism?

Table 6.1 Team development audit tool

	Notes	Team attributes
A purpose, value base and sense of direction that is meaningful to its members		
Objectives that integrate with the plans of the wider organisation and are regularly reviewed		
Trusting relationships between its members and positive regard		
A climate where problems can be raised and practice challenged		
Responsive and flexible leadership that encourages participation		
A good range of personalities and roles		
Procedures and ways of working that allow it to work effectively including resolving conflicts		
Good relationships and established working relationships with co-providers		
Good relationships and established working relationships with the rest of the organisation		
Continuous team development and improvement		
Good communication within and outside of the team		

- Am I sensitive to other people's feelings?

- Do I take on my share of responsibilities willingly?

- Am I honest and say what I think and feel?

- Do I generally trust other members of the team?

- Do I try to dominate the conversation?

- Am I willing to support other people's ideas?

- Am I tolerant of opposing viewpoints?

- Can I tolerate silence?

- Do I help tasks get completed?

(Source: Thomas *et al.*, 2009b)

Your team as a source of support

So far we have explored how you might contribute to the effectiveness of your team. However, it is important to remember that your team is also a crucial support for you. Being part of a team can be very rewarding personally, but it can also offer you some crucial practical help. Let's return to Liz our newly qualified social worker.

CASE STUDY **6.2**

Cycling without stabilisers: the experiences of Liz, a newly qualified childcare social worker in a statutory agency

I completed my three-year social work degree through the employment based route. I already knew the team that I joined as a newly qualified social worker as I worked in the team during my course when I wasn't on placement. When I returned at the end of the course as a newly qualified social worker there had been a high turnover of staff so I didn't know as many people. I was the new girl, although fortunately I knew where the toilets were, whose cup not to use and where the stationary cupboard was.

The team were very welcoming but I didn't have an induction and from day one I had my own caseload of real live families and children in need. I had previously been a family support worker so working with families wasn't too daunting. However, it was a big transition to discover what my role as a newly qualified social worker really was. I had been a confident, maybe even a bit arrogant, social work student who was doing and learning new things every day on placement, writing about theories and practice, knew the law inside out, and was supported every step of the way by lecturers, practice teachers and placement supervisors. Suddenly I was a newly qualified social worker with a supervisor who was really supportive but drowning in paperwork and procedures and squeezing in supervision where she could. It was like someone had taken the stabilisers off my bike. Although it was exciting to start 'real' cycling I kept falling off and there weren't people right next to me to pick me up. I had to look around to find someone. I found the biggest support came from family support workers and professionals from other agencies like health visitors and teachers. Suddenly I was the newly qualified social worker who they welcomed as part of their team.

ACTIVITY 6.3

Liz uses a powerful analogy of learning to cycle and found that she needed people to 'pick her up' when she fell.

Take some time to consider who might be able to offer support and encouragement to you in your team and how you might build a relationship with them.

As Liz described, these people may not be other qualified social workers, but colleagues working alongside or nearby in other roles. They may well not even be in your organisation. Adams (2005) reminds us of social work's distinct and sometimes unique contribution to working with other professions in multi-disciplinary teams and it is not just the effectiveness of our immediate teams but also these wider teams that have an important impact on service quality. They are often described as interprofessional, multi-disciplinary or inter-agency teams. This important theme of interprofessional and inter-agency collaboration is explored in more detail in Quinney *et al.* (2009), Thomas *et al.* (2009a, 2009b) and Whittington *et al.* (2009a, 2009b). However, these wider teams not only have a lot to offer us both personally and as practitioners, they also present us with their own challenges. So what do we need in order to be an effective member of a multi-disciplinary team? A good starting point is a strong sense of professional identity.

Professional identity as a newly qualified social worker

An important aspect of surviving and thriving in your new job is that of professional identity. Although you have recently qualified as a social worker you may not be clear about what distinct contribution you will be able to make to the team you have joined (see Chapter 7). You may have asked yourself how other people in the team see you as a social worker and also how people who use services, carers, and the general public see you. You may be feeling apprehensive as well as feeling excited and relieved to finally be working as a social worker after the demands and rigours of the qualifying course you have recently completed. This will be particularly so when you are practising in an interprofessional or inter-agency context.

A study by Keeping (2006) identified several things that social workers can do to sustain their professional identity when working in interprofessional and inter-agency settings. You may find these helpful in overcoming initial uncertainties about your new role and your status as a newly qualified social worker.

These are:

- staying connected to your professional community – through regular contact with other social workers;
- staying connected with your practice and sense of purpose – through a reflective approach to your work and the values that underpin it;
- seeking clarity about your role and validation of your contribution – through discussions with colleagues and in supervision;

- enlisting the help of managers – through acknowledging and challenging appropriately when organisations policies or procedures have a detrimental impact on professional practice.

Keeping (2006, p 33) uses extracts from interviews with social workers, some of them reflecting back on their experiences of being newly qualified social workers, to illustrate her findings.

> *. . . one of the difficulties with social work itself is that its aims are quite diverse, so it's quite difficult to describe to outsiders what you do exactly . . . just thinking back to when I started, I guess in my first jobs I didn't have a very clear idea of what I was doing.*

and

> *social workers need to be clear about what they are doing . . . they need to be clear about their own aims as a profession. When I first started out, I remember there being a big discussion about what social workers do within mental health teams and somebody reeling off a big thing about social workers don't take referrals from psychiatrists, they don't do X,Y,Z . . . I don't think you can define yourself by what you don't do.*

(Keeping, 2006, p 33)

CASE STUDY **6.3**

Liz's top tips for developing your professional identity

- *Find yourself a mentor whether this is a senior social worker, someone in senior management, a lecturer or practice teacher. Someone who you respect, who understands the nature of social work and can give you direction on a wider scale. I approached an area manager who had been with the local authority for over 20 years. He gave me insight into the organisation, encouraged me to think beyond just being a social worker and recommended other things I could get involved in as well as encouraging me with the skills I already had.*

- *Don't be scared to ask for help. If you look as though you are coping that's what people will think.*

- *Look after yourself. Easier said than done, but really important for those who want to be a social worker for the long haul. Establish clear boundaries. Turn your work phone off and don't look at work emails when you get home. Establish good habits right at the start, if you start off planning to have a lunch break you are more likely to have one.*

- *Establish a good work pattern so if you're rubbish in the mornings then don't try completing an assessment at that time. Just because a colleague may prefer to get in at 8am you may work better till 6pm.*

- *Don't compare yourself. Just because your colleague always gets their assessments completed on time and you struggle to, it might be that you manage a crisis situation well or are good at establishing good relationships with people who use services and other agencies.*

- *Get organised. Buy yourself a filofax with a zip so you can keep pens and pieces of loose paper safe or, if technically minded, an electronic organiser. Your diary is an*

CASE STUDY 6.3 *(CONT.)*

important tool and if you learn to manage it you will be more flexible when things don't go as planned. Book in future appointments and meetings in advance. That way you have a clearer picture of how much time you have left.

- *Learn to prioritise, or ask someone to help you, particularly when everything seems important.*

- *Establish good working relationships with other agencies. Book in time before or after meetings to discuss your roles so differences can be ironed out.*

The points being made here are very important. It is important to prepare for interactions with other professionals and people who use services and carers by being clear about the remit, services and powers of the agency you work for, your role and the role of others and to be able to explain this positively. This will help you and them feel better informed and enable others to have confidence in your interactions with them.

It can be helpful to refer to the International Federation of Social Workers' (2000) definition of social work when you want to feel engaged with a sense of purpose for social work that has resonance in many countries across the world:

> *The social work profession promotes social change, problem solving in human relationships and the empowerment and liberation of people to enhance well-being. Utilising theories of human behaviour and social systems, social work intervenes at the points where people interact with their environments. Principles of human rights and social justice are fundamental to social work.*

> (International Federation of Social Workers, 2000)

The extent to which social justice can be realised, if at all, through the efforts of individual social workers in the UK is contestable. Arguably, however, it is this political dimension which distinguishes social work from other professional groups. It is also important to hold on to the importance of values in social work practice. *Values determine who we are and how we practise: what we do, how we do it and why we do it* (Warren, 2007, p 71).

In order to stay connected to your sense of purpose, you may also find it helpful to reflect on what it was that led you to become a social worker in the first place. In a study of people wanting to become social workers and a review of the current literature, Moriarty and Murray (2007) found that the opportunity to *make a difference* was the main reason for people wanting to work in public sector services and that life experiences, altruism and idealism are other influencing factors. In another study, Gilligan (2007) looked at how social work applicants see the origin of and solution to social problems. Values are inherent in motivations and how people define social problems. Also, people's responses to situations are influenced by them.

If you are interested in reading more about the career paths and motivations of social workers you may like to read the collection of thirteen accounts of social workers in the UK engaged in practice, management, and education settings (Cree, 2003). These narrative accounts will help you to consider the range of possible routes within social work and may inspire you in your future career path.

If a clear sense of professional identity and purpose is essential to being an effective member of a multidisciplinary team, what else can help?

Professional differences and similarities

In exploring professional differences and similarities, Whittington (2003) suggests that what can help is trying to understand:

- what we have in common;

- what we can each contribute distinctively;

- what is complementary between us;

- what may be in tension between us.

Using the above bullet points together with Table 4.2 in Chapter 4 will help you maintain a critically reflective approach to your professional identity and practice. What else might help?

Creating networks and making alliances – the other 'investing in people'

The organisation you are working for may have a logo on their official paperwork and website that marks them out as having achieved the 'Investors in People' standard. This standard involves meeting evidence indicators on developing strategies to improve the performance of an organisation; taking action to improve performance of the organisation and evaluating the impact on the performance of the organisation. To read more about the standard visit the Investors in People website **www.investorsin-people.co.uk**.

We will now explore other forms of investing in people, involving developing networks and alliances with colleagues and other significant people and to the importance of working in a learning organisation (Gould and Baldwin, 2004).

Both formal and informal networks which cross organisational boundaries can contribute to transforming practice. The aim is to not only have the support of the frameworks and line management systems within the agency or organisation, but to be able to establish and draw on a wider range of people through local networks and contacts whose skills, experience and local knowledge can be drawn on to make services more responsive to individual and local need.

Adams (2005) points to a study in the USA by Sarason and Lorentz (1998) in an education setting. The study identifies *people with a flair for boundary crossing as a key to effective co-ordination* (Adams, 2005, p 12) and this has important messages for newly qualified social workers. Adams (2005) also highlights social work qualities and skills in their findings, that contribute to effective boundary crossing, partnership working, creative and transformational practice. These are:

- developing real and authentic knowledge of the locality or subject area, driven by 'curiosity' and a proactive approach to learning;

- being readily alert and recognising commonalities, using imaginativeness;

- a strengths-based approach which recognises assets;

- being able to appropriately use power and influence and selflessness.

Brechin (2000, p 37) urges critical practitioners to create connections with other professionals *through which real communications can occur, bringing opportunities to learn about others' views and perspectives and discovering ways of talking constructively about differences of opinion.*

Good communication, therefore, is also crucial in co-ordinating services to ensure that they meet the needs of people who use services.

Good communication – the key to effective inter-professional practice

Several research studies have drawn attention to the obstacles experienced by people who use services and carers, of ineffective collaboration between professionals and agencies and highlight recommended improvements, for example:

> *Many [service users and carers] valued good communication, both between members of staff, and between staff and service users . . . Users and carers commented on the importance of knowing that staff shared information, and therefore had a better understanding of the user, viewing them as a 'whole person'. They were more confident of receiving the right care if staff were communicating with each other.*

> (Miller and Cook, 2007, p 64)

Case study 6.4 is a first hand account by a carer of some of the problems encountered when working with several professionals and agencies involved in the care of his wife.

CASE STUDY 6.4

A carer's experience

I have cared for my wife over the last 13 years and especially since she was diagnosed with a personality disorder. We have four children.

My experience of multi-disciplinary teams in this example is based on the last nine months and many of the issues I talk about below have yet to be resolved – it's an ongoing saga shall we say!

At the beginning of 2008 my wife admitted herself into hospital and stayed in for about two weeks. Toward the end of her stay there was a discharge planning meeting with the consultant, a ward nurse and the two of us – there was no Community Mental Health Team member, even though it was planned to discharge her later that day. My wife had asked for the follow up meeting not to be during school finish time, but nobody listened – they arranged the meeting when our children were coming back from school.

My wife's GP, Children and Family's Social Worker, Community Mental Health Nurse and Consultant were invited to a follow up meeting to discuss her care. Neither her GP nor the allocated social worker could attend. My wife was then referred to a new Consultant, one who is an expert in personality disorders. He met with her, compiled an in-depth report on the basis of this meeting and her notes, and set up a multi-disciplinary review meeting.

Letters were again sent out to her GP and the Children and Families Social Worker. By ringing the Children and Families Social Work team up I found out that they had not been informed that she had been discharged from hospital! Her Social Worker had also changed. Her GP didn't attend or reply to the invitation letter. Nevertheless the outcome of this review meeting was that they gave my wife three options – and needed another meeting to discuss them as my wife would not attend the meeting.

This is where we are today. It's been hard work – we are getting somewhere but what we've been through highlights the need for, and the importance of, good communication. The care co-ordinator, whoever that might be, plays a crucial role as a broker between a person who uses services, their carer and other professionals.

ACTIVITY 6.4

What are the challenges and opportunities for you as a newly qualified social worker if you were to find yourself in this situation?

Accepting that, as in this case study, some obstacles will be hard to overcome: think about different techniques or strategies you might use to enable clearer communication between colleagues in different organisations and between professionals, carers and people who use services.

Managing the tensions created by inter-professional practice

Sometimes there can be real tensions and conflicts in interprofessional practice that are about more than effective communication and demand from us different stances and different skills.

- Being calmly assertive is an important skill to practise. There will be occasions when you will need to ask for clarification about the views and activities of other professionals in order to improve the experiences of people receiving services, and your knowledge about working with other professionals will help you do this with more confidence and authority. For example you might be in a situation where you need to question the attitudes of another professional about age or race or about a judgement that may appear to place a person who uses services at risk. Perceived or structural hierarchies of status and power need to be recognised and overcome to promote clear and open communication.

- Whittington *et al.* (2009a) point out that several studies (Hudson, 2002; Lymbery, 2006; Townsley *et al.*, 2004) have shown that historical differences in professional status and the ways in which services are organised can lead to territorial attitudes to professional boundaries. The relative status and power of different professions can also lead to tensions and inflexibility. Lymbery (2006) highlights the importance of social workers challenging the 'dehumanising' aspects of other services that older people may experience.

- Working with other professionals and agencies can also be time consuming as additional time has to be allowed for reaching a consensus in decision-making, and for co-ordination (Penhale, 2007). From the viewpoint of carers and people who use services, the discussions between professionals may take place over their heads and exclude them (Turner *et al.*, 2003; Beresford, 2007), so you may need to be very active in order to include and empower them.

- In addition to clear communication, a range of studies have pointed to the need for good leadership, management, supervision, and staff development to support effective collaborative working (Whittington *et al.*, 2009a, b). As a newly qualified social worker you will have limited levels of influence in some of these areas but it is important that you are assertive about your development needs in supervision meetings and that you participate in formal and informal staff development opportunities.

- When working with other professionals we have to ensure we understand each other's viewpoints as well as those of the people who are the focus of the assessment and their carers. Sometimes the perceptions of needs, strengths, and risks by people who use services and carers, can be in opposition to one another and may also conflict with the views of professionals (Quinney *et al.*, 2009). Effective care management demands that you attempt to reconcile some of these differences and broker a way forward.

- These experiences will inevitably be compounded by wider structural inequalities for example in relation to gender, class, race and disability. So you may need to actively challenge discriminatory behaviour.

ACTIVITY *6.5*

Take the assertiveness quiz in Thomas et al. *(2009) (see the SCIE web-site) and make a note of and take action on the feedback from your score.*

Remember, the person with the widest range of behaviour options is likely to be the most successful in any communication (McBride, 1998, p 7).

Before finishing the chapter let us just remind ourselves of a particular strength you will bring to your new teams.

Helping your team develop research-mindedness

Remember Liz the newly qualified social worker at the start of this chapter who identified the many strengths that she took to her new team? Several of these related to the fact that she was an effective and up to date researcher. This 'research- mindedness' can be really important to a team, as practice on qualifying courses has often got ahead of practice in the field. So as a newly qualified social worker it is an area where you may be able to make a valuable contribution. What is research-mindedness? It has been described as:

93

- a faculty for critical reflection informed by knowledge and research;

- an ability to use research to inform practice which counters unfair discrimination, racism, poverty, disadvantage and injustice, consistent with core social work values; and

- an understanding of the process of research and the use of research to theorise from practice (Centre for Human Services Technology, undated).

Your experience of having developed research skills and awareness during your qualifying course of how research can inform or transform practice should continue to be built on and applied in your practice.

As Dominelli (2005, p 226) tells us, research has many purposes in social work as it can be used to:

- enhance the status of the profession in both the field and the academy;

- improve services by finding out what people who use services think about those that have been delivered to them;

- evaluate the extent of their use and who uses them;

- highlight issues;

- elucidate depth and complexities in practice;

- explore problems;

- raise additional questions; and

- enhance critical reflection.

As a social work student you will have been familiar with the importance of accessing and evaluating research and applying it to practice situations in your assignments; and as a newly qualified social work practitioner you will be able to extend these skills and knowledge in order to apply research findings to your everyday practice, but also to undertake research into practice and to more systematically evaluate your own practice. Humphries (2008) reminds us of the need for commitment and passion underlying being research-minded when this involves enquiring into the inequalities and injustices that people who use services experience.

How is the use of research promoted and encouraged? According to Walter *et al.* (2004, p 13) this involves:

- ensuring a relevant research base;

- ensuring access to research;

- making research comprehensible;

- drawing out the practice implications of research;

- developing best practice models;

- requiring research-informed practice; and

- developing a culture that supports research use.

It is useful to take time to find out about the culture of the team or organisation in relation to research minded practice. Talk to people who are doing research, find out what practical support there is to undertake research and find out about the facilities for accessing research information.

One of the things you will have relied on, and possibly taken for granted, while at university was the vast range of materials a modern university library provides you with access to, in many cases by using an *Athens* password. You will have been able to borrow library books and access the contents of peer reviewed journals in addition to the learning resources available through the course's virtual learning environment. Unless you are registered on a programme of study, perhaps a post-qualifying award, you are unlikely to have access to a university library – either physically or electronically, so you will need to be resourceful and search more widely for material. It will also be important to 'make friends' with your computer terminal – you'll spend a lot of time together. These computer and information technology skills will be important not only for searching for information and research but a large part of a social worker's time is spent inputting data into computer systems.

ACTIVITY *6.6*

Publicly available sources of research and literature to inform practice include resources available electronically from the following.

- *Social Care Institute for Excellence* **www.scie.org.uk**.
- *Joseph Rowntree Foundation* **www.jrf.org.uk**.
- *Your agency may have access to Research in Practice* **www.rip.org.uk**.

Did you know? As a member of the British Association of Social Workers (BASW) you are eligible for a preferential personal subscription to peer reviewed BASW journals, the *British Journal of Social Work* and *Practice: Social Work in Action.* A subscription will enable you to remain up to date with academic and practice-based research and ideas.

Summary of key points

- Remember the many strengths you are bringing to your new team.

- Actively seek to build trust with your new colleagues.

- Reflect on how effective your team is and try and contribute to its development.

- Work on improving your contribution to team meetings.

- Multi-professional working presents many challenges. Develop your sense of professional identity and work on understanding, collaboration, communication and assertiveness.

- Your 'research-mindedness' is an important asset that you bring to your team.

I would like to end the chapter with some positive encouragement from Marion, a Strategic Director of Children's Services who has a wealth of experience as a social worker, manager and head of service.

CASE STUDY **6.5**

Marion's advice

Even though the reality is that you will be working with chaotic and difficult families, focus your energy on the things that are known to produce the best outcomes for children and young people, making good use of the support and expertise of your team and other professionals. Despite what you might read in the newspapers, social work is still a fantastic job.

FURTHER READING

Payne, M (2000) *Teamwork in multiprofessional care.* Basingstoke: Macmillan.
Payne provides a useful resource for learning more about working in teams.

www.resmind.swap.ac.uk (Accessed 24 March 2009)

To learn more about being research minded in social work visit the above 'research mindedness' website. The aims of this very user friendly learning resource are to:

● help you understand what being research minded means;

● assist you in assessing your current level of research mindedness;

● provide you with a range of resources for improving your research mindedness;

● support you in developing research-mindedness amongst fellow students, colleagues and other stakeholder partners or collaborators.

www.scie.org.uk/publications/elearning/index.asp (Accessed 24 March 2009)

To learn more about interprofessional and inter-agency collaboration visit the website of the Social Care Institute for Excellence (SCIE) and view or download the soon to be published series of e-learning resources devoted to interprofessional and inter-agency collaboration written by Quinney *et al.* (2009), Thomas *et al.* (2009a/b) and Whittington *et al.* (2009a/b).

The resource titles are:

● *An introduction to interprofessional and inter-agency working.*

● *Professional identity and collaboration.*

● *Building relationships, negotiating trust and negotiating with others.*

● *Assessment of risks, needs and strengths.*

● *A model of practice and collaboration.*

● *Working collaboratively in different type of teams.*

● *The practitioner, the agency and inter-agency collaboration.*

Chapter 7

Contributing to service quality and development

Ivan Gray, Jonathan Parker and Marian Macdonald with a contribution from Liz (person who uses services)

This chapter will help you to meet the following National Occupational Standards for Social Work.

● Key role 5, unit 15: contribute to the management of resources and services.

The current chapter also links with the previous chapter concerning collaborative working and helps you meet:

● unit 17: work within multidisciplinary and multi-organisational teams, networks and systems.

Introduction

As a newly qualified social work practitioner you may sometimes feel alone in your role. In reality though, you are always part of the bigger team, including all the people in your organisation that support your work and the network of interrelated services with which we work in partnership. This is even the case for people practising as independent social workers. The quality of your individual practice and the way people who use services experience it, will always be affected by this broader context in which your work is set. This impact can be experienced as positive or negative. So, for example, if you set up a care planning meeting and the administrative team get the invitations out too late and key people do not attend, the quality of your practice is diminished. If you put together a care package with people who use services but their day-care provision is poor, your assessment work and the rest of the plan may be undermined. Where services do not work together, people who use services may experience an inadequate and fragmented service that not only does not respond to their needs but can even confuse or damage them. On the other hand, good systems, relationships, and service provision can greatly enhance your practice. For instance, an effective family support service or a specialist assessment can much enhance your work. Volunteers and supportive local leisure facilities can greatly improve a care package and ready access to training and developmental activities can improve the quality of your practice.

Individual practice cannot really be distinguished from organisational practices. Rather, we are perhaps best seen as members of a *community of practice* (Wenger, 2006), in which our individual perspectives, aspirations, and actions form part of these wider systems and relationships and, in social work, these are underpinned by our explicit value base (see GSCC, 2004). This makes influencing the broader context in which your practice is set central to high quality professional practice, and starts with helping the different systems communicate and work together, but it can go beyond this.

The National Occupational Standards for Social Work in England (Topss England, 2002) emphasise the need for you to contribute to the development of services and to maintaining service quality. Unit 15 identifies the need to: *contribute to the management of resources and services* and describes four key activities:

Unit 15.1: contribute to the procedures involved in purchasing and commissioning services.

Unit 15.2: contribute to monitoring the effectiveness of services in meeting need.

Unit 15.3: contribute to monitoring the quality of the services provided.

Unit 15.4: contribute to managing information.

Unit 17 expects you to: *work within multi-disciplinary and multi-organisational teams, networks and systems* and as part of that work describes two key activities:

Unit 17.2: contribute to identifying and agreeing the goals, objectives and lifespan of the team, network or system.

Unit 17.3: contribute to evaluating the effectiveness of the team, network or system.

On placement it is often hard to be able to do justice to these standards, and it is not unusual to find that social work students tend to focus on developing their own practice and take, as given, the broader context in which it occurs. So, as a newly qualified social worker, contributing to service quality and development is likely to be a key area for personal development and for this reason it is the subject of this chapter. Before exploring this important area of work it is worth making a few observations.

Learning organisations and 'distributed leadership'

Chapter 4 has already explored how important it is to services that you continue to develop professionally throughout your career. Your effectiveness as a practitioner is dependent on your effectiveness as a learner and it is fundamental to your continued registration to be involved and document your learning post-qualification (see pages 59–64). Yet your practice will always be dependent on the resources, systems, procedures and relationships of the organisation in which you work, and the network of provision in which it operates. Personal expertise is not enough, so that beyond your continuing professional development lies the issue as to whether organisations are continually 'learning'. Do they seek continually to improve the quality of the services they provide or do they simply repeat past mistakes and failings? The importance of developing 'learning organisations' has been recognised in *Options for Excellence* (DfES/DH, 2006). The Social Care Institute for Excellence has introduced a model designed to help an employer develop the characteristics of a learning organisation (SCIE, 2006a, 2006b).

The biggest block to developing a learning organisation is perhaps the power relationships that stop people contributing to problem solving and decision making. This has led to the development of the concept of 'distributed leadership' (Watson, 2002; Mehra *et al.*, 2006); responsibility for the leadership and management of the service is distributed as widely as possible within the organisation, mobilising the full expertise and the abilities of all staff to innovate and lead. In effect, in an organisation practising distributed leadership, everyone is a leader or manager.

Distributed leadership is more readily practised in an organisation employing social workers because they will have developed expertise and responsibility for the effective leadership and management of their cases, so it is not as hard to reach beyond this and engage them in the broader endeavour of effective leadership and the management of services. This perspective, of distributed leadership, determines the aim of this chapter – to start the process of you developing your leadership and management skills so that you can contribute to the broad development of service quality.

But will I be allowed to get involved?

Perhaps a big question you may ask is: will my agency or organisation allow me to be involved in service changes and development? Your contribution to the development of service quality may not be fully facilitated by your organisation. A criticism of current service provision is that we suffer from 'managerialism' (Jones *et al.*, 2004) which is viewed as the imposition of centrally determined agendas that do not allow for the involvement of staff in service development and improvement.

On the other hand, if we find all our contributions encouraged, welcomed, and implemented we would already be part of a learning organisation. Indeed, we would have arrived. Rather we are all part of a work in progress, so contributing fully to service quality and development is necessarily aspirational. This schism between managerialism and distributed leadership constitutes a polarity that needs bridging (Johnson, 1996). Managers need to offer social workers more scope to contribute and staff also need to reach out and embrace managerial perspectives and issues. You may find this challenging as it demands grappling with the acknowledged resource constraints and demanding policy initiatives, such as the participation agenda (DH, 2007), that may require significant changes in your practice.

Whatever your circumstances, empowered or struggling against the system, it may not be possible to promote our social work values that commit us to providing services that are as responsive as possible to the needs of people who use services, without addressing the issue of service quality and improvement. If we sometimes find our circumstances to be daunting, and the impact we might have limited, it is worth remembering that small changes can make a big difference. Tom Peters, the 'managing for excellence' champion once suggested that some of the biggest service improvements can be small ones (Peters, 1989). He uses the example of a significant service improvement resulting from a team moving a filing cabinet; having worked around it for the last two years. He suggests it was a massive step forward – not in the least because the team had at last felt empowered enough to do it.

It is also worth remembering that as an agent of service improvement, a social worker is particularly well positioned. Apart from people who use services and their carers, (who are the closest to the issues), you are well placed to identify and respond to problems. You will also be gaining understanding of your organisation, how the system works (or not) and how to influence teams, managers, and other groups that make up the service. You are a crucial 'broker' between management, the wider organisation, networks of service provision, and those that use them. You not only negotiate and secure an individual's care package; you also have the potential to broker available services and their quality (see Figure 7.1).

Herein lies an important point; if distributed leadership suggests that leadership should be diffused as much as possible within an organisation, it also raises the question as to whether it should be distributed to people who use services. This is the thrust of the current participation agenda, allowing users to lead and manage their own services (DH, 2007). As a social worker you will play a key role in engaging both people who use services and carers in service improvements through identifying problems, designing improvements, and implementing solutions. For example, this can be achieved by evaluating the effectiveness of services they receive or working with representatives of people who use services, using their expertise to bring about service improvements (see Liz's Case Study 7.1). To ensure this involvement is genuine will require you to challenge, question and change your practice and to seek to change your organisation.

CASE STUDY 7.1

Liz's involvement in service development

Involving the public, users of services and carers, in health and social care development initiatives has been increasingly promoted in recent government policies in the UK and is high on the agenda of regulatory bodies (DH, 2002; DH, 2006; Lowes and Hulatt, 2005).

My own experience of involvement has developed over many years; from being a silent voice at a formal strategy meeting, to participation as one of many stakeholders; and now to an expert in my own field. As a user of mental health services, I wanted to do something positive to 'make a difference.' Initially, I was thrust into an alien environment which excluded me through its structures and jargon. The professionals did not know what to do with me. I sat at a meeting and then left. To continue, I had to question my purpose and function.

Through a user forum, I began to accept invitations to speak about my experiences. I spoke to others so that I could offer a balanced perspective of how people experienced services. I came to conclude that often what people were offered was 'service led' rather than 'needs led'. I wanted to communicate that the voice of the 'consumer' was key. Receiving a service, appropriate to individual need made sense and was surely more cost effective? My aim was not to be critical, but to simply report 'how it is' and offer constructive input on how it could be better – for both the practitioner and person using services. The practicalities of being involved proved to be a challenge. These included:

- *being required to attend meetings at 9 am which involve a long journey by public transport;*

> ## CASE STUDY 7.1 (CONT.)
>
> - *having no prior discussion/training to be able to participate from an informed perspective;*
> - *waiting months to receive any payment for expenses;*
> - *finding myself sat next to my own Psychiatrist at a service review!*
>
> *It is only by voicing these difficulties that change can occur. It is not always easy when fluctuating mental health can bring periods of acute anxiety and withdrawal. In spite of this, I have worked hard to gain respect and credibility in my involvement activities and have begun to engage in meaningful dialogue with all stakeholders. I am encouraged when I have tangible evidence that I have been heard and taken seriously.*
>
> *The gains of involvement are rarely financial, so what motivates me? I want services to be of a high quality and to provide good outcomes for those who use them. I want to use my years in the system in a positive way; to give something back. Through this, my confidence and sense of self-worth have significantly increased.*
>
> *I started out as the token user of services – wheeled in and out at the appropriate time and my involvement was meaningless. This has developed into what I would describe as inclusive and productive partnership working.*

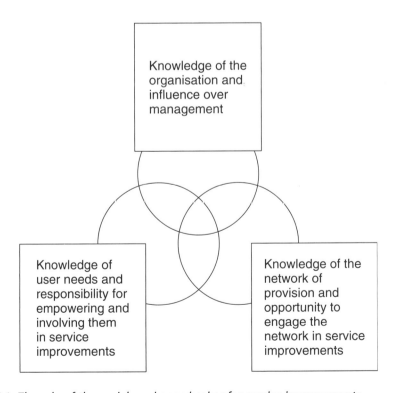

Figure 7.1 The role of the social worker as broker for service improvements

101

So what are your options: how can you get involved in developing services?

There are a number of options open to you as a newly qualified social worker to become involved in the development of your organisation and service.

- In your everyday work you can seek, with your team, to make immediate improvements in working practices when dealing with individual cases or systems that affect service quality.

- You can take responsibility for championing a particular aspect of a service, developing particular expertise and sharing this with your team.

- You can identify, in your every day work and in supervision, quality issues and solutions to them that would enhance services or even new ways of working – and then get these on the team agenda.

- You can lead, or be a member of, a project team or working party designing or implementing a service development that has been delegated to you.

- You can contribute to, or lead, auditing and business planning initiatives to generate improvement plans (although this may be a little later in your career than immediately post-qualification).

CASE STUDY 7.2

James and his multidisciplinary team

Since qualifying six months ago, James has been working as a social worker in the Grange, a multidisciplinary team for adults with physical disabilities. He recognised that formal supervision sessions were undertaken according to and by particular members of the professions represented in the team. He was new to working in such a multidisciplinary environment and was eager to learn about what others did within the team. So, he suggested a monthly lunchtime meeting in which a member of each discipline would discuss how they would work with a particular case and opened this to others. This allowed workers to share and understand the different perspectives of the team and engendered a greater degree of trust across the team.

All the above options are dependent on how effective you are as a problem solver. Taking a problem solving approach to your work is the key to contributing to service improvements, to the development of your team and the wider organisation. So, what is effective problem-solving?

A problem-solving approach

Charles Handy (1993) describes managers as 'organisational GP's' – they diagnose and then prescribe treatment plans that deal with organisational disorders. They investigate problems with service quality, formulate, and implement solutions. In a distributed leadership approach everyone seeks to improve service quality, but how can we maximise our effectiveness as problem solvers? The problem-solving process is outlined in Figure 7.2.

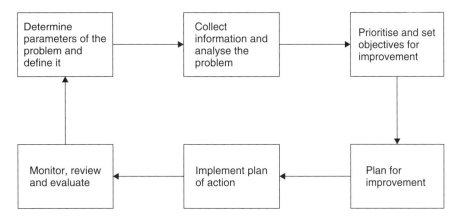

Figure 7.2 The problem-solving process

This cycle of activities can be described as at the heart of leadership and management – a logical and rational approach that brings order and control to any process. Central to the management of any task, the problem-solving process appears in many guises. It can also be called the decision making process or the planning process – there are many variants. In social care we might re-badge it as the case planning or assessment process, while in other professions it appears as the teaching or the nursing process. The challenge is not to develop a completely new set of knowledge and skills but rather transfer knowledge and skills you already use as a case manager and apply them to services more generally. In leadership and management, this process can be applied to just about any activity area; for instance, slightly re-framed it becomes 'the business planning process' (see Figure 7.3).

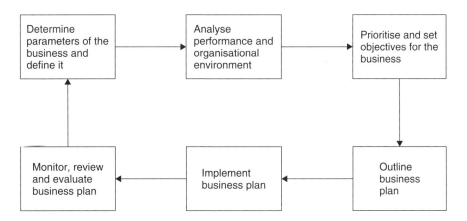

Figure 7.3 The business planning process

An important aspect of problem solving, as illustrated by Figures 7.2 and 7.3, is that the process is 'iterative'; there is a feedback loop that allows progress to be reviewed and changes made to problem definition and analysis. Sometimes this process is presented in a linear fashion (see Figure 7.4).

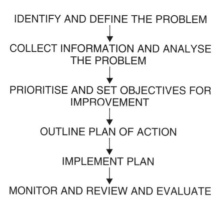

Figure 7.4 A linear representation of the problem-solving process

Although the lack of a feedback loop in this linear representation is a disadvantage, it does have its uses. It does offer a logical structure to a written report, and could shape any recommendations you might make if you are leading or contributing to a working party exploring a quality issue. This way of working may be quite familiar to you as a newly qualified social worker, and similar to the processes you are involved in when working with cases. Transferability of learning and skills is something that you will be become quite adept at.

This process can also be used more pro-actively, such as the basis for project management (see Figure 7.5). Rather than identifying a problem with the delivery of an existing service, it can be used to introduce new service developments.

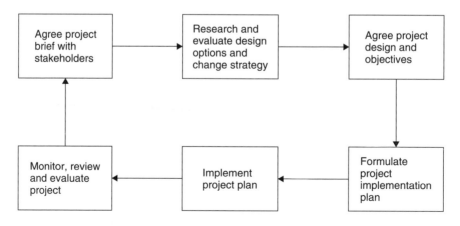

Figure 7.5 The project management process

James and the day centre

James had been discussing the services provided at a day centre attached to his office with members of that centre. They were requesting more overt involvement and a users' forum. James discussed with centre members what that forum would be like and took his ideas to his next supervision with his manager. James agreed to consider what happens in other day centres and to use his research skills from his degree to search for information on similar projects, and to take a view from those who used the day centre on the best way forward. After discussing a range of options he took a plan back to his manager and set up a forum in which all who wished to could be involved and have a say in addressing issues of concern; feedback on services offered and present ideas for future activities and projects to develop. James' manager supported him by acting as a facilitator and conduit for people using the day centre to develop the service. When his manager suggested to him he was involved in project management and developing the service, James said he simply thought he was working with those using the day centre to enable them to make choices. He had not thought that the two could be the same.

The problem-solving process, like most models, is necessarily a simplification. Reality and application can be more complex and more problematic. Hamm (1988) describes the different levels of problem solving as a cognitive continuum (see Table 7.1).

Table 7.1 Levels of problem solving

Judgement	Problem solving
Individual judgement	You apply problem solving process to a case or situation using your professional knowledge and expertise to determine a response.
Peer-aided judgement	Your assessment is agreed by your supervisor or your report and proposals become the basis for a care plan as the result of a multi-disciplinary planning meeting.
Systems-aided judgement	You follow a process determined by experts and organisational/professional experience that helps you problem solve (e.g. child protection and risk assessments, and flow charts used by advisors at a single access point).
Quasi-experimental	Pilot projects and action learning groups where a group methodically analyses a service issue and adjusts activity on the basis of findings.
Scientific research	Problem solving where there is a clear systematic research methodology, structured information collection, verifiable analysis, and the presentation and dissemination of findings and/or outcomes.

Based on Hamm (1988)

Accepting that you may get involved in problem solving at all levels, let us explore each of the stages in turn and then discuss some of the broader issues.

Problem identification and definition

Applying the problem-solving process can take up a lot of resources. Therefore, direct your activity towards priorities. A useful rule for thinking about this is Pareto's 80:20 rule (MSH and Unicef, 1998). This suggests that 80 per cent of breakdowns in service quality lie with 20 per cent of the problems. Try to identify these *key* problems, rather than those that will actually have little impact on overall quality. Quality assurance systems can help identify and quantify service quality problems; business plans can generate priorities for improvement; and risk analysis can also be used to determine priority problems. Many organisations have also developed complex risk assessment processes that can help identify where services might break down (Bostock *et al.*, 2005).

The clearer the problem definition the more focus can be given to problem analysis, objective setting, and planning. The greatest clarity comes from being able to quantify the problem. Performance measures, so often maligned but more often misunderstood, are designed to help you do this. Just think how difficult it would be to determine whether change had taken place if you and your user of services had not agreed on specific measures that would indicate this? Performance measures are useful when considering organisation and agency priorities as well.

Collecting information

It has been suggested that in war and in management the easier information is to come by the less useful it is. A problem needs researching thoroughly, including identifying and agreeing on what constitutes evidenced-based practice and sometimes interviewing stakeholders. Information collection and exploration in social work and social care can be as complicated as full blown social research and, as such, it is time consuming and expensive.

Often, we will operate with insufficient information, having to make judgements on the basis of what is available at the time. This can prove more costly in the long run, but in a crisis we often have little choice. In general, however, planned and methodical information collection impacts positively and directly on the effectiveness of problem solving. It is worth remembering that the crucial information you may need to solve a problem could lie in the experiences of those stakeholders who are involved in the problem. Engage them in problem solving and you immediately improve the quality of your information collection.

Analysis

Problems vary in their nature and demand different approaches to analysis. So, for instance, it may be possible to accurately measure and use statistical analysis to identify the causes of some problems. Yet, many problems faced by social work practitioners and managers cannot be analysed in this way and demand qualitative approaches. A combination of approaches is often necessary. To illustrate; if you want to improve the percentage of assessments completed within a timescale set by a performance measure, you may wish to interview a small number of staff to identify possible causes for delays. Then you might carry out a survey across the service so that you can target the dominant causes. Analysis can embrace a number of activities and can be very multifaceted, especially in complex social situations. Some options are shown in Box 7.1.

BOX **7.1**

Options for analysis

Applying social science – social science provides us with a range of different explanations for human behaviour. Each can cast a different light on an issue and also suggest a different response (Cunningham and Cunningham 2008; Ingleby, 2006).

Applying social work methodologies – the different social science approaches have generated different social work methodologies and interventions. These can readily be mobilised to help you analyse management problems and interventions.

Applying models of good practice – sometimes there are models of good practice that can be used to compare current practices against (see Skills for Care, SCIE and Social Policy and Social Work (SWAP) web sites – **www.skillsforcare.org.uk**, **www.scie.org.uk** *and* **www.swap.ac.uk**.

Using standards and benchmarks – it is increasingly the case that desirable behaviour is defined by the production of detailed standards. An example of this is the national management standards from the Management Standards Centre (MSC, 2005). These can be used to judge not only individual performance but the general performance of a particular activity. So, for example, the supervision unit could be used to set development objectives for an individual manager or audit performance across a service (SfC/CWDC, 2007).

Analysing the change environment – analysis needs not only to address the problem but the capacity of individuals, work teams and organisations to implement change and how the change might be managed effectively and successfully (DCSF, 2006).

Systems analysis – if organisations or services are viewed as interacting social systems, then analysis should approach problems as multidimensional and caused by the interaction of several systems, all of which may need to be addressed. Part of analysis should also explore the impact of an intervention in one part of the system on the system as a whole. Otherwise a solution in one area may create a problem elsewhere (Fish et al., 2008).

Action learning and appreciative enquiry – it is possible to work with a team helping you analyse a problem and identify possible causes or build on strengths and competencies to bring improvement (Hart and Bond, 1995).

Setting objectives

A common approach to objective setting and planning is that they should be SMART.

- S – specific;
- M – measurable;
- A – achievable;
- R – realistic;
- T – timely.

(See Parker and Bradley, 2007, pp 65–67, for an application to social work planning.)

This is a popular formulation which was and still is contrasted with a tendency in social care to be inexact, or to focus on the 'art' rather than the 'science' of social care. As a mnemonic it has value but should not be used slavishly as, 'process' as well as 'outcome' objectives do matter; particularly in a value orientated activity like social care. To demonstrate, an objective such as: *To ensure that stakeholders are committed and motivated in implementing the change*, is not 'SMART' but it might be crucial in determining the success of the service improvement. One could argue that it could be made measurable, but this might be an unnecessary effort that does not do justice to the qualitative nature of the objective. It certainly will not be hard to reach for evidence that stakeholders are engaged and motivated.

It is important to remember that objectives serve two crucial purposes. They structure both planning and evaluation. Each objective should have a plan of action that are the actual steps that will be taken to achieve it, and monitoring may focus on the implementation of this plan of action. Evaluation should involve a review of each objective. Objectives can have different priorities. Some may need to be identified as 'success criteria' and can be separated out, as such, to provide the crucial measures against which a problem solving activity or project can be evaluated.

Plan of action

As we noted previously, it should be possible to link each element of a plan of action to an objective or objectives. A simple plan identifies what will be done, who will do it, and when they will do it by. However, there are more complicated planning methods such as bar and Gantt charts that can assist with planning more complex implementations and facilitate monitoring (see Walker *et al.*, 2008 for a review of useful management tools in practice education). There are also opportunities here to identify creative ways of achieving objectives, rather than relying on standardised responses. Involving your team and other stakeholders in planning can often generate creative options and builds commitment.

Risk analysis can be used to identify and gauge the possible causes of breakdown in an improvement project. Sometimes, when a risk is judged to be considerable a contingency plan can be developed that can be quickly put in place when a problem is identified.

When broad, alternative options for achieving an objective are identified techniques, such as a decision-making matrix, can be used to try and make an informed judgement about the best way forward.

It is good practice to include an objective that encompasses the monitoring and evaluation of any implementation. This should be planned for in advance to avoid the tendency to leave evaluation to the last minute and to do it badly, thereby excluding any huge gains that can be made from learning from mistakes. As a newly qualified worker, the more time spent on planning, the better. It will help you to identify success and see where things do not always work as planned. In this way, you can monitor your progress and development.

Monitoring and evaluation

It is all too common *not* to monitor evaluation. This can have a number of unfortunate outcomes, including the stalling of any implementation. It is essential to determine who will monitor, and how. Early identification of difficulties in implementation can often lead to timely resolution. Disruption or re-thinking should be planned into the work.

Monitoring can be aided by establishing milestones. These are key dates along the 'journey' of implementation that pinpoint when crucial activities will have been completed. This gives a welcome structure to monitoring, and a project or development team can use these 'way marks' to meet and consider progress and respond to problems.

Evaluation is a review of a project's effectiveness. It should explore each of the objectives in turn, as well as asking whether the problem as a whole has been responded to or whether the aim of the project has been achieved. Any evaluation can raise insights to inform other developments within an organisation. In other words, it is as essential as the problem solving process is to the functioning of learning organisations. As implementation or work on the problem or project is likely to be ongoing it can allow for re-analysis and the setting of new objectives and a new plan. In effect, it allows us to learn from experience and continuously improve services.

Going beyond objectives and performance measurement: evaluating service outcomes

It can be argued that while it is important we try and measure activities, perhaps by target setting, success criteria, and performance measurement, a potentially negative impact may be that the real purpose of changes and improvements are lost. This has led to services attempting to reach beyond measurable outputs to 'service outcomes'. This can be at an individual, community, or societal level and demands thinking further than whether a child's needs assessment was carried out on time and according to the relevant performance criteria to evaluating the impact of the assessment in respect of meeting their needs and improving their long term quality of their life. The next stage beyond this would be to ask if the range of services provided were having a wider social impact in enhancing the quality of life of a community.

Evaluating service outcomes is much harder than identifying if objectives have been achieved or measuring outputs (e.g. how many assessments were provided). Going back to Table 7.1 and the different levels of problem solving, determining service outcomes can involve us in complex, long-term and expensive social research. Yet it is important that we try and reach beyond the numbers to the features of a service that really determine its quality.

How do you monitor and evaluate your own work?

Think about your own work as a newly qualified social worker. Write down some of the ways you monitor and evaluate your work. Consider what you have learned when you evaluate your work and what you have learned when you have not evaluated your work.

Remember, effective evaluations:

- *are planned;*
- *evidenced;*
- *explore the overall aim of the intervention, each objective and any success criteria;*
- *involve key stakeholders;*
- *are the basis for personal and organisational learning and development;*
- *try and evaluate service outcomes.*

If you are interested in learning more about service evaluation and the political and participatory functions it can have, try reading Everitt and Hardiker (1996), Rossi et al. (2004) and/or Unrau et al. (2007).

Some issues arising from the problem solving process

The problem-solving process is not, of course, a panacea. It will not solve all problems you may face in working in, leading, and developing organisations. Some common objections follow.

It oversimplifies: it can be argued that the basic model (Figure 7.2) oversimplifies reality and that in practice actual problem solving is very different. For instance, things don't happen stage by stage. Information comes in all the time leading to changes in analysis, plans and objectives – in an altogether much more fluid process.

We argue that it is important to use a simple model to help order our thinking and actions and, of course we accept that all models by their nature simplify to provide structure. Accepting that the actual process of assessment is more complicated, with a practitioner moving flexibly around the cycle. This does not mean that a formal analysis, objectives and agreed plans are not necessary.

It's too positivistic and too individualistic: the approach can be seen as assuming a knowable objective reality that can be analysed and changed rationally. An alternative interpretation often cited in social care is that meaning is created by people, so that the process of negotiating the definition of a problem, agreeing objectives and a plan of action are more important than 'scientific' analysis.

This may be the case in public services, where there could be several stakeholders with different problem definitions, analyses, and objectives that have to be recognised and reconciled. However, the importance of mobilising groups and communities as problem solvers could be seen as the pathway to effectiveness in any organisation. Senge's (1990) formulation of a learning organisation emphasises the importance of group problem solving as does total quality management and theories of Communities of Practice (Wenger, 2006). Case planning meetings, reviews, and case conferences can all be seen as exercises in group problem solving. For instance, a good chairperson is likely to consciously try and follow the problem solving process, encouraging people to share information and analyse it rather than jumping straight to a possible plan of action.

Need for a double feedback loop: Argyris and Schön (1978) suggest the need for a double feedback loop to achieve critical problem solving (see Figure 7.6). That is to say, the culture of an organisation influences the problem solving process so that everyday identification of problems and responses to them are standardised and based on hidden assumptions that define culture – *the way we do things around here*. A double feedback loop challenges these value assumptions and power relationships: e.g. who defines the problem; how it is defined; how are causes identified; how are objectives prioritised; which systems are not challenged; which plans are eventually adopted; and whether carers and people who use the services have been consulted and involved? Although limited resources can restrict options considered in the plan of action, the feedback loop can also be used to challenge the efficacy of the process itself e.g. was the definition of the problem clear enough; were enough sources of information used; and to what extent was the analysis critical?

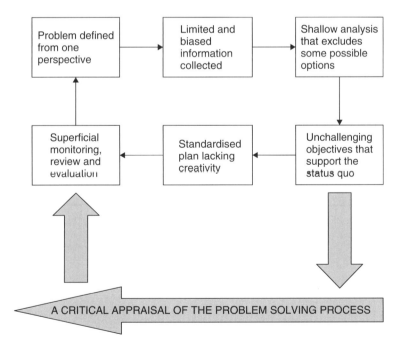

Figure 7.6 A double feedback loop

Learning styles and problem solving: According to your learning style (see Chapter 4, pages 48–49) you might be seen to emphasise different parts of the problem solving process to the detriment of others. For instance, a theorist might enjoy the analysis, a reflector review and evaluation, a pragmatist the planning, and an activist the implementation. Effective problem solving, and therefore effective leadership and management, may demand a balanced style. This critical self-awareness can be seen as an extension of the double feedback loop and encompass questioning how your personal history and value base might influence your approach.

Applying the problem-solving process to your team or unit

Unit 17 of the National Occupational Standards for Social Work, as outlined at the beginning of this chapter, expects you to contribute to team development and team planning. Team development involves developing the ability of the team to respond to whatever it might be faced with and to improve its systems processes and relationships. Or if you like, it is about building the capacity of your team. Although we have already touched on this issue in Chapter 6 it is worth noting that team planning is often now called business planning and is about determining the objectives the team seeks to achieve.

The problem-solving process can underpin any methodical approach to managing an activity. What often varies is the analysis. So if we explore team or business planning, and refer again to Figure 7.3, the second box, 'analyse performance and the organisational environment', will probably be your biggest challenge as a newly qualified social worker. The factors you can draw on in this analysis are outlined in Figure 7.7.

There are a number of things to note in how we have represented Figure 7.7.

- We have emphasised the involvement of all stakeholders. Each has a part to play in the service either as contributors or beneficiaries. Not only are they the best source of information but are crucial in agreeing and implementing any future plans. People who use services are the most important stakeholders.

- Making judgements about previous organisational performance involves collecting information. Some are readily available as performance measures but some will need collecting as they arise e.g. out of supervision.

- As a team you will need to keep abreast of national policy initiatives.

- Your manager will play an important role of feeding you organisational information to which you may not have ready access. There may be local organisational strategies and service plans that you need to incorporate into any business planning.

- You will probably need to carry out some benchmarking activity such as reviewing team performance against service standards like the Commissioning Standards that can be accessed on the CWDC (**www.cwdc.org.uk**) and Skills for Care (**www.skillsforcare.org.uk**) websites.

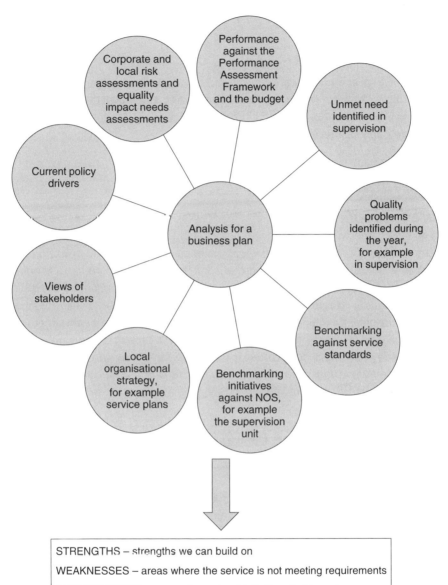

Figure 7.7 Analysis for a business plan

- Some 'good practice models' are worth considering (see following section on learning organisations).

- We suggest that the different factors feed what is often called a 'SWOT' analysis to identify key objectives that, as in Figure 7.3, are translated into the detail that becomes the team's business plan.

- If you and your team are not ready or able to get involved in a full business planning process then try and identify a simple team service improvement plan to which you can all contribute. Sometimes, once you start reviewing some aspects of service provision and thinking about options that might bring improvement, it can become part of how a team works and can develop over time.

CASE STUDY 7.4

A carer's support group

Karla was concerned that her new team never really looked at the gaps in locally available services, but based care plans on what was assumed to be there. She believed there could be a much wider range of services and that some big gaps could be filled. In supervision, she began to identify what she thought were unmet needs and talking about projects she had become involved with on placement as a student or knew colleagues had been involved in. Her team manager started exploring this in supervision with others and after discussion in a team meeting it was suggested that a carers' support group would be valuable. Karla and others pointed out it was important to be sure what carers wanted and she started working with a colleague to talk to carers about what might be developed locally to offer them more support.

Are you working in a learning organisation?

As we move toward the end of this final chapter, it is important to address an issue we raised earlier. Another approach to contributing to service quality is to develop your team and organisation as a learning organisation. A learning organisation mobilises all its resources to continually learn and develop itself. The Social Care Institute of Excellence (SCIE) have developed an audit tool that is designed to help us develop our organisations as a learning organisation. There is an adapted version of this audit presented as Box 7.2 after the final case study. You can use these questions with your team. It is worth noting that you may, as Zoe found out (Case Study 7.5), draw different conclusions in analysing your team as compared with the wider organisation. You may end up with an improvement agenda for your team that includes the need to influence the wider organisation. Reflect on how this might be usefully deployed in meeting your development needs in contributing to organisational and agency development.

CASE STUDY **7.5**

Learning organisations

Team meetings had got rather 'flat'; the dynamism had gone and people began to miss them. Zoe's manager mentioned this in supervision and said she was looking at ways of 'livening them up a bit'. Zoe suggested they use the SCIE learning organisational audit to review how they worked as a team. They sent off for the SCIE cards and used them to generate debate in a team meeting. The discussion got a bit heated, but the team were reminded of the many things they did well as well as finding some areas where they could make improvements. They concluded that they were more of a learning community than the wider organisation. Her manager thought she might take these findings to the management team meetings despite being a little unsure how well they would be received.

BOX **7.2**

Learning organisation audit

On a five-point Likert scale ranging from strongly agree to strongly disagree, rate how the following statements apply to the information systems used in your organisation.

- *There are effective information systems for both internal and external communication.*
- *The organisation makes good use of IT to improve information exchange and management.*
- *Information is freely available.*
- *Where possible, information is shared openly with people who use services and their carers.*
- *Policies and procedures are meaningful and understood by all.*

  Using the same Likert scale rate how the following statements apply to the structure of your organisation.

- *Feedback and participation of people who use services and carers is actively sought.*
- *Team working, learning and utilising all staff skills are integral to the organisation.*
- *There is cross-organisational, collaborative and partnership working.*

  Again, using the same Likert scale rate how the following statements apply to the culture of your organisation.

- *There is a system of shared beliefs, values, goals and objectives.*
- *Development of new ideas and methods is encouraged.*
- *An open learning environment allows the opportunity to test innovative practice.*
- *New evidence and research are considered and incorporated into practice.*

- *Ideas and proposals can come from any part of the organisation – not just 'top down'.*

- *People who identify problems are not blamed.*

  Again using the same Likert scale rate whether the following statements are present in your workplace.

- *There is a commitment to continuous personal and career development for all staff and by all staff.*

- *Individual learning styles and learning needs are responded to.*

- *A good range of formal and informal learning opportunities are open to all.*

- *A high quality of individual supervision and support is offered.*

  And finally, using the same Likert scale, rate whether the following leadership strengths are established in the organisation you work for.

- *The organisation develops and improves services wherever it can.*

- *Leaders model the openness, risk-taking and reflection necessary for learning.*

- *Leaders ensure that the organisation has the resources and capacity to learn, change and develop.*

- *Learning and development opportunities are linked to organisational objectives.*

  These statements have been adapted from the SCIE website and are used with permission within this book (see SCIE, 2006).

Summary of key points

We hope the perspectives we have presented in this chapter will help you build on your professional skills and increase your influence over service quality and development by being able to contribute more to the leadership and management of services. We know that some of you will find that your organisation does not encourage you to play a full part in this, but you will always be able to make some improvements and may find some ways forward by which you can help them change features of their culture that are unhelpful and move towards achieving the features of a learning organisation.

Whatever your experience, we hope you share with us the perspective that service development cannot and should not be separated out from professional practice. This means that leadership and management skills are core professional competencies and that they should feature strongly in your continuing professional development. The essence of empowerment and distributed leadership is also perhaps best seen as the involvement of people who use services and carers in the leadership and development of services. At the very least this should involve opportunity to play a part in leading their own care plan, but their potential and the potential of our services will only be fully reached when they are enabled to contribute to building service quality and determining the future of services more generally.

Everitt, A and Hardiker, P (1996) *Evaluating for good practice*. Basingstoke: Macmillan.

This small book offers a critical and value-based approach to evaluation of social work services and individual practice in the UK. It recognises the complex political settings in which social work is practised.

Walker, J, Crawford, K and Parker, J (2008) *Practice education in social work: a handbook for practice teachers, assessors and educators*. Exeter: Learning Matters.

This is a book written specifically for practice educators. It examines contemporary theories and knowledge in practice learning, teaching and education, with a clear emphasis on developing the skills and practice of individual social workers performing these roles.

Appendix 1

What is assessment?

Jenny Bigmore and Penny Lodwick

This appendix will help you to meet the following National Occupational Standard for Social Work.

- Key role 1, unit 3: assess needs and options to recommend a course of action.

    Assessment is a core skill in social work and should underpin social work intervention.

    (Crisp *et al.*, 2003, p 1)

    Assessment is not a single event; it is an ongoing process, in which the client or service user participates, the purpose of which is to assist the social worker to understand people in relation to their environment. Assessment is also the basis for planning what needs to be done to maintain, improve or bring about change in the person, in the environment or both.

    (Coulshed and Orme, 2006, p 24)

Assessment will be something that you will have been given an introduction to, as part of your qualifying course. However, assessment skills need to be developed over time as your experience and knowledge base grows. Once you qualify and take up your first social work post, there will be an expectation that you will have an understanding of the complexities of undertaking an assessment and the importance of developing your skills, beyond information gathering towards a more critically analytical approach drawing on an evidence base of theory and current research in your specialist area of practice (e.g. see Brown and Rutter, 2008).

Lord Laming commented in the Victoria Climbié Inquiry Report (Laming, 2003) on the social worker's lack of inquisitiveness.

    While I accept that social workers are not detectives, I do not consider that they should simply serve as the passive recipients of information, unquestioningly accepting all that they are told by the carers of children about whom there are concerns. The concept of 'respectful uncertainty' should lie at the heart of the relationship between the social worker and family. It does not require social workers to constantly interrogate their clients, but does involve the critical evaluation of the information they are given.

    (Laming, 2003, p 205)

The types of assessments which you will be required to undertake will vary according to your work setting. They will be introduced to you within their own specific legal and policy frameworks and should be accompanied by guidance and relevant training. For example, *The Framework for the Assessment of Children in Need and their Families* (DH, 2000) is accompanied by extensive guidance and tools, such as questionnaires and scales. However, these are *only* tools and can be relatively ineffective if not utilised in a thoughtful and critically analytical way.

As part of the process of identifying important areas for practice development for newly qualified social workers we have sought the views of social work managers and their experience of where assessment skills need to be improved and developed. One service manager and former team manager working in Children's Services, makes the following comments.

> *In the analysis of serious case reviews (Brandon et al., 2008), it talks about practitioners being encouraged to be curious and to think critically and systematically. This sums up my thoughts. I would add that observation skills are also key, particularly in the questioning and evidence building stage. Often, less experienced and/or less confident practitioners are really good at collecting vast amounts of information but struggle with the analytical task and do not always make the links between past events and separate factors which can interact to either increase or decrease risk or conversely the ability to protect. I am often surprised at how practitioners readily accept information provided by parents and/or adults at face value with a degree of naivety or false optimism. I think that important assessment skills are the ability to constantly question, hypothesize and process information, recognising where there are gaps and how significant that missing piece of the assessment jigsaw can be. For me, good assessments seek to question, support and/or evidence the information provided by families (and other professionals too of course). Practitioners need to be able to challenge discrepancies and/or contradictions.*

> *Another skill is the ability to revise or review an assessment in light of new information, incidents and/or developments. I think that sometimes assessments become too 'set in stone' and don't get adjusted according to new information. The ability to compile and use chronologies to identify trends is key in this respect. Taking into account past history and being aware of the tendency to adopt the 'start again syndrome' was also identified in the serious case reviews and is a key assessment skill (Brandon et al., 2008).*

A guide to incorporating analysis in assessment

As a part of your qualifying social work training, you will have been introduced to the concept of assessment and hopefully had the opportunity to start to build on this skill during practice placements. However, it is only when you start to practice as a newly qualified social worker that you begin to build your specialist knowledge base which will inform the assessment process and assist in your critical analysis of the information gathered.

For the purposes of this guide we will use *The Framework for the Assessment of Children in Need and their Families* (DH, 2000) as an example of how to utilise an assessment framework. However, the skills and knowledge required are transferable across disciplines and could be applied to a variety of assessment frameworks.

> *An understanding of a child must be located within the context of the child's family (parents or caregivers and the wider family) and of the community and culture in which he or she is growing up.*

> (DH, 2000, p 11)

If we take this statement as the starting place when allocated the task of undertaking an assessment, it clearly places the child at the centre of the assessment, but highlights the importance of exploring the relationship that the child has with other systems with which the child has either direct or indirect contact.

In the guidance (DH, 2000), this is represented using a triangle (see Figure A1.1) with the child in the centre, and the three sides of the triangle representing different domains.

- The child's developmental needs

- Parenting capacity

- Family and environmental factors

Rose (2004, p 40) notes that:

> *The Assessment Framework represents a way of trying to capture the complexity of a child's world and beginning to construct a coherent approach to collecting and analysing information about each child.*

What we know from research is that social workers are quite good at information gathering, particularly in the first two domains (the child's developmental needs and parenting capacity) and appear less rigorous in gathering information in the third domain (family

Figure A1.1 The assessment framework (adapted from DH, 2000, p 89)

and environmental factors) (Calder and Hackett, 2003). A further area that often creates difficulties, particularly for newly qualified practitioners is . . . *Now I've got all this information, what do I do with it and what does it mean? Is it reliable and do I need to know anything else?*

We can acknowledge that the framework is based on a systems framework or theory, but what does this mean in practice?

A systems framework is used to examine the mutual influences that the child, family, friends, neighbours, community and wider society have upon one another (Jack, 2004, p 54). The important words to pull out here when analysing information are *mutual influences.*

Why?

In order to understand how different factors impact on the child in terms of current risk and future outcomes, we need to understand how all of these factors are interconnected. For example, if a feature of a case is a parent who misuses drugs, you would need to look at how the drug misuse impacts on the three different domains of the assessment triangle in order to assess the impact on the child. The issues below represent *just some* of the topics you might consider in the above example.

A child's developmental needs
- The impact of any prenatal exposure to maternal drug use in terms of development and any special needs arising as a consequence.

- The impact on school attendance and educational outcomes.

- The impact on attachment relationships.

- Is there a protective parent/carer – issues of resilience and risk?

Parenting capacity
- What impact does the drug misuse have on the parents' ability to parent the child?

- How does it impact on their availability both physically and emotionally to parent their child?

- What strategies do they have to protect the child from their drug use, such as access to drug paraphernalia?

- Patterns of drug use.

Family and environmental factors
- What is the level of engagement with drug treatment services?

- Is there a support network outside of the home?

- What is the nature of the support network? Does it involve other drug users?

- Issues around offending behaviour.

- Impact on home environment and financial resources.

Your analysis will be evidence-based, using a foundation of knowledge which draws on theory, research and practice experience in order to make sense of the interaction between the different factors which impact on the child. For example, you can ask the following questions.

- What does research say about the impact of drug misuse on parenting?

- If a parent is emotionally unavailable to a child, how does this impact on attachment relationships and future outcomes?

- What are the risks around chaotic drug use?

- If the drug using parent is not engaging with services, why not?

Answers to these questions will form part of your analysis and inform the planning process for intervention and services. For example, information about why the parent has not previously engaged with services will influence decisions about what might be most appropriate. Knowledge of the types of service available will inform these decisions too. You are not expected to know everything, but must know where to seek the advice and information you require. Working with other agencies is a fundamental part of undertaking a thorough assessment and will assist you in making sense of the information gathered.

It is important to view the evidence and information gathered, *critically.* This means not just taking the information at face value. Ask yourself, is the source reliable? Do you need any further information? Have you spoken to everyone that you need to? If there is more than one child in the family, have you considered the impact of parental drug use on each individual child and not just made assumptions that they will all be affected in the same way? This will be informed by your knowledge of theories of child development, taking into account issues such as age and stage of child development, as well as an understanding of issues of resilience and risk. Have you considered the issues from the perspective of the person using services, not just from your own? Asking and answering this type of question during the assessment process will help you to plan services to meet need.

> *It is essential that practitioners review the information they gather and use the knowledge from research to move beyond descriptions of why a situation has occurred. From this, they can plan services to meet need and safeguard children.*

> (Seden, 2007, p 4)

We end this appendix with a suggested way forward for you to develop your assessment skills.

BOX A1.1

A suggested way forward on assessment

Revisit a good, introductory text book. You should have already accessed one as part of your qualifying course. As a newly qualified social worker you will now have some prac-tice experience to apply it to. Parker and Bradley (2007) provide a very accessible, general introduction to assessment, planning and review – we recommend you focus initially on the first two chapters. Keep your eyes peeled for further forthcoming Learning Matters texts on assessment too.

SCIE (2007) has also produced a resource guide on assessment in social work: a guide for learning and teaching. Although it has been written for educators it provides an excellent starting point (Whittington, 2007) – it is available from: **www.scie.org.uk/ publications/resourceguides/rg08/teaching/index.asp** *(accessed 29 January 2009).*

The National Occupational Standards for Social Work (available from **www.york. ac.uk/depts/spsw/documents/3SWNOSdocpdffileseditionApr04.pdf** *(accessed 29 January 2009) include assessment in a number of the key roles. Revisit the key roles and look specifically at the knowledge base highlighted for each key role in relation to your specific area of practice and start building on these. Building the evidence base which underpins your practice and informs your assessment is a continuous process and involves keeping up to date with current issues and research.*

We would strongly advise newly qualified childcare practitioners to read the Framework for the Assessment of Children in Need and their Families (DH, 2000), paying particular attention to Chapter 4: Analysis, Judgement and Decision Making (this document can be accessed electronically on the Department of Health Website – **www.dh. gov.uk/en/Publicationsandstatistics/Publications/PublicationsPolicyAndGuidance/ DH_4008144***) (accessed 29 January 2009).*

Appendix 2

Care management and contracting

Brian Jones

This appendix will help you to meet the following National Occupational Standard for Social Work.

● Key role 5, unit 15: contribute to the management of resources and services.

Starting work as a newly qualified social worker in my day felt like you now had your licence to get on with it. At the end of the 1970s modern social work was asserting itself and the relatively new but rapidly developing Social Services Departments were becoming a confusing environment for social work team managers. These managers were often old hands from Children's Departments who had undergone one year 'emergency' training courses and who now struggled to cope with expanding responsibilities and a wave of swaggering young men and women, newly qualified and ready to take on the ills of society.

My Certificate of Qualification in Social Work course had been two years in length, had no examinations and no grades for essays (just a pass or fail) and the politically motivated amongst us had infused the process with Marxism. The world was going to change and our society with it and we could promote that change by stepping into a social work post in a local authority or social work agency.

So what has changed in 30 years for the newly qualified social worker? Society has changed but perhaps not as was envisaged. Post-Thatcherite Britain has retained an ambivalent relationship with social work whilst the management revolution has come to local authorities bringing the 'target culture' and a heavy emphasis on budget control. Some would say that social work itself has had to 'come of age' in an attempt to explain itself and to be accountable in this type of environment. As a social worker today you will now be accountable to a professional body, your employer, and people who use services, but there is still no reason to suppose that this should compromise your unique skills and core values which must be enshrined in practice.

As a newly qualified social worker your extensive period of specialist education and training will provide the springboard for your career, but you will be diving into the organisational culture and procedures of your employer. That employer and organisation, whether a public body or a third sector agency, is likely to be short of money and confused about its ambitions as it is buffeted by the demands of central government and the levels of demand from people who use services. You and your colleagues, with your unique combination of academic understanding and day-to-day 'hands on' experience, can be a powerful influence in this scenario.

When joining your new organisation it is not unusual to become dismayed by the apparent mass of policies and procedures threatening to bear down on your task. Policies and procedures, like legislation, cumulate over time. Traditionally, social workers have had to distinguish between those policies and procedures that are 'live', and so needed for the task, and those less visited. I suspect that this has not changed over the years.

In my experience, the day-to-day work of a social worker is not overly academic but research always has its place and can vary from useful small scale local work, often available from students to larger scale work, commissioned by senior managers aimed at reviewing policy and procedures in answer to a perceived demand, or available via national websites such as **www.rip.org.uk**.

You will undoubtedly hear much talk of 'care management' and 'contracting' in the world of practice. Care management came to us with the NHS and Community Care Act 1991 and, initially, referred to the methods and style of working that should be adopted in order to provide costed 'care packages' (those funded by Social Services) to individuals in order to prevent them having to move on to a care home. Prior to care management we supported people by using what 'in-house' services were available together with the use of local knowledge and some use of grant-giving Trusts and other charitable organisations. This approach was often simply too little, too late and care management opened up a whole new set of services and possibilities. In the role of care manager you will join your user of services at the centre of a web of support services paid for by the Community Care budget and you will be in charge of the monitoring of its effectiveness and the cyclical review process. Social work teams had long ago solved the problem of people getting lost in large bureaucracies by adopting the case management method of working. Care management added cash (often with a cash limit for procuring services for any one person using services) as a means of obtaining services from independent organisations and on a contractual basis from the voluntary sector.

With care management came the contracting culture. The average Social Services Authority now obtains (or 'procures' in contracting-speak) over 50 per cent of its domiciliary care service from outside organisations, as well as much of care home provision. Millions of pounds are spent this way and so we have had to develop skills in commissioning and contracting. Each council with social services responsibilities now has a 'Commissioning and Contracting' section. Commissioning is the process of identifying the social care needs present in a population and procuring services to meet those needs. This is another cyclical and endless process. Contracting is the procedure that underpins the procurement by specifying the service that is required from an individual provider organisation (often just 'provider') and the price that has been agreed for units of the service. Get commissioning wrong and vulnerable people will suffer. Commissioning cannot be effective without accurate data from the front line and you are about to go to the front.

Good commissioning and contracting enables you, as care manager, to assess an individual's situation with them and propose 'packages of care' designed to assist, support and, where possible, re-enable.

Care management generally consists of four major stages in a cycle.

Assessment (see Appendix 1) is where you will enter the world of the person in need. I very much enjoy this stage because it requires a combination of social skills, observational and investigatory skills, and advocacy all backed by social work's firm value base. Assessment also will often require work with practitioners from other professions to achieve a multidisciplinary assessment. You will get this right if you can find a way to work with the people in the situation in a way that they find acceptable and provide the insight and facts that will allow you to satisfy procedural requirements and, more importantly, reveal what the situation 'turns' on. Get this part right and you have all you need for the second stage.

Care planning is where you analyse the data or reflect carefully on that situation often with others, be that your team manager or peers or, in some places, team members from other professions. The outcome should be a set (or sets) of proposals for actions that will improve the situation for your user of services. If you do this well your person who uses services will meet your proposals with some enthusiasm, or at least, informed acceptance. Good care planning is firmly based on the view of people who use services, of his or her situation and on his or her desired outcome. This is often difficult to achieve not least because of possible attitudes adopted by his or her relatives and the likelihood of a shortage of resources.

The third stage is the setting up of the 'package' and the monitoring of its impact on the situation. The services at your disposal in setting up the package will depend on the effectiveness of your organisation's commissioning and contracting arrangements. Good commissioning will have a procedure for acknowledging gaps in provision and you will need to report any problems with availability or quality of services, so that efforts can be made to overcome those deficits. As you will be dealing with someone's life and any package may involve several elements (services or agreements with people who use services, carers and family members) monitoring may need to take place over weeks or even months to establish the effect of the package.

Review (sometimes Case Review) is the fourth stage. A review is where all the information (from all the participants and legitimate stakeholders) on the situation and efforts to improve it are brought together so that judgements can be made on effectiveness and suitability for the future. Very often adjustments are decided upon and you will communicate these and make the arrangements. Doing this well requires good communication especially as reviews are seldom full scale, formal, face to face meetings but rather review sessions with your manager, the effectiveness of which will depend on the veracity of the information that you supply and your ability to convince your team manager of the extent of the need to go on spending on the particular situation.

Care management is best thought of as a framework within which much social work takes place and there is almost always a way to assert your own style of social work. Social Work Departments are now challenged to improve continuously. Most recently 'personalisation' of services has become the rallying cry. For social workers of an earlier generation this appears as a reaffirmation of social work principles and practice, because of its re-emphasis of the service user's wishes, and yet will require a combination of good management and commitment and innovation from today's social workers to fire the organisational development to make this a reality.

Moving from studying social work to practising social work full time will be a challenge but nowadays you will have a team manager who is now much more likely to talk your language whilst possibly having some skills in the dialect of the organisation's corporate body or governing committee. This means that you are less likely to be told simply *that's how things are done around here* and more likely to receive a resume of where various issues are at the moment and the progress on proposals and plans for development, including an invitation to take part in all this.

Now, no less than ever, we are going to need all our talent and all our effort at working together to meet the challenge of society's ills. So if you have that commitment and believe in our ability to innovate, cooperate and remain true to our social work values, you may just have chosen the right career.

Appendix 3
Court skills

Clare Seymour

This appendix will help you to meet the following National Occupational Standard for Social Work.

● Key role 5, unit 16: manage, present and share records and reports.

In our research the key issue that stands out above all others in the advance of newly qualified social workers' learning needs is the development of court skills (Bates *et al.*, 2009). The following article describes a model to support the development of these skills and is written by Clare Seymour. It is reproduced with her kind permission and that of the original publisher, copyright Whiting and Birch, from the *Journal of Practice Teaching and Learning*, volume 7, pages 70–81, in 2006/07. Although the article was originally written with practice assessors or educators in mind, its excellent content is equally pertinent to newly qualified social workers. In fact, this content is based on a much more detailed text published by Learning Matters in 2007, *Courtroom Skills for Social Workers* by Seymour and Seymour (2007). This book contains useful advice, research summaries, case examples, websites and further reading sections and is strongly recommended as the starting point for this demanding aspect of a newly qualified social worker's journey.

A model to support the development of courtroom skills

There is widespread interest on the part of social work degree students in developing their courtroom skills within a framework of learning about social work law, but it is often not until they qualify and are 'thrown in at the deep end' that anyone gives any serious thought to the need for preparation and skills development in this area. As a result, students and newly-qualified social workers are frequently apprehensive about court work, which means that they do not always do themselves, or the people who use social work services, justice when faced with court involvement. This article offers a model for practice assessors to use with students in agencies where court work is undertaken, and encourages skills development against a foundation of critical analysis and reflection. The term 'practice assessor' has been adopted by the General Social Care Council in preference to the previously widely-used term 'practice teacher' to describe the person responsible for facilitating learning and supervising and assessing social work students in practice. Within this model, 'practice assessor' is interchangeable with 'practice teacher', and indeed most of the suggested learning activities primarily involve a facilitative or teaching, rather than an assessment, role.

Keywords: social worker, social work students, courtroom skills, model for skills development, observation and shadowing, reflection, evidence, cross-examination, values.

Introduction

Law is a key area of teaching and learning in the social work degree. Knowledge of legal rules and skills in their application are included in the social work benchmark statement (QAA, 2000) and in the knowledge and key role requirements of the National Occupational Standards for Social Work. However, most commentators agree that the relationship between social workers and lawyers in practice is often strained, characterised by antagonism and distrust, and that social work students frequently approach learning the law with fear and lack of confidence (Preston-Shoot *et al.*, 1998, cited in SCIE, 2005). Many qualified social workers also experience court work as extremely stressful, which can result in defensive practice in which the values of their profession appear to become sidelined or obscured. The courtroom is an arena where preparation and rehearsal is difficult, and yet frequently court work is where the robustness of social workers' practice, professional confidence and knowing the rules can make a key difference to the experience of people who use social work services (SCIE, 2005, p 174).

Preston-Shoot (2000) suggests that competent practitioners are those who are:

- confident (to challenge);

- credible (in presenting the rationale for decision-making);

- critical (to make their practice and legal rules accessible to those with whom they work, to assess the impact of policies on people's lives and to navigate through questions of ethics, rights and needs);

- creative (in order to exploit the possibilities that legal rules present and to manage the practice dilemmas and conflicting imperatives that the interface between law and social work practice generates).

Cull and Roche (2001) further argue that health and social welfare professionals do not need to learn to *think like a lawyer*, but instead to engage with the complexity of the law-practice interface. This encompasses factors such as the values and principles which shape the two professions, and the motivation and personal attributes of their respective practitioners. Also important are the differences in the nature of the relationships which lawyers and social workers have with their clients and in the structure and regulation of law and social work, and the frequently negative influence of preconceptions and stereotypical assumptions. The comprehensive SCIE review on the teaching, learning, and assessment of law in social work education (2005, p 49) emphasised the need for social workers to develop the conceptual tools to understand law, rather than simply learning what the law says. These principles can only be developed against a practice framework in which students feel able to question, challenge and debate issues which arise in the legal context of social work.

The SCIE review found that courtroom skills were, for the most part, not identified specifically in social work education, but tended to be included in generic learning objectives, such as *being confident in using the law* and *understanding the legal system.* Despite, or perhaps because of, apprehension about court work, there is evidence of considerable interest in the part of social work students in developing their knowledge and skills in this area. When Anglia Ruskin University introduced an elective module on courtroom skills as part of its social work degree, the module was heavily oversubscribed and well-received. However, as with any area of learning, knowledge, skills and values have to be applied to be effective, and practice assessors in agencies where social workers regularly undertake court work can play a key role in helping students develop and apply relevant skills, such as keeping up-to-date with changes in law and policy, advocacy, communication, fact-finding and research, writing and presenting reports, presenting an argument, using facts to formulate an opinion, problem-solving, negotiation and responding to challenge. There is evidence, too, that learning about the law is often not retained (Preston-Shoot *et al.*, 1997, cited in SCIE,2005), and it is suggested that this may be because academic learning is *insufficiently linked to practice, failing to connect the law and social work, or to engage students on a personal level with the context of what they are learning* (SCIE, 2005, p 30). It follows, therefore, that practice assessors are in a key position in which to maximise the effectiveness of students' learning.

It is possible for students to undertake academic preparation for court work, by, for example, researching the historical development of the courts, the structure of the legal system, court rules, legal language and concepts, and there are many accessible texts available to facilitate this. However, without practical application, such information is likely to prove difficult to understand and retain. This model offers a framework with which to support students in developing confidence and competence in court settings.

Reflecting on attitudes to the law

As preparation for professional involvement with courts, students should reflect on their own experiences and consider how these may influence their current attitudes to courts and lawyers, and their understanding of the legal system. Sitting on a jury, ending a marriage or partnership, being convicted of a motoring offence or having to wind up a relative's estate will each shape perception and understanding of legal processes and the people involved, which in turn can influence professional behaviour. Comparing their attitudes towards lawyers with those they have towards other professionals will help students identify the preconceptions they hold, and form the basis for devising creative ways of overcoming the barriers which can impede effective professional relationships.

Law reports appear in the *Times* on most days when the High Court is sitting. Other newspapers usually publish them weekly, and they are available on various websites (**www.lawreports.co.uk**). Encouraging students to keep any cuttings which relate to decisions in cases within their particular areas of interest will give them a flavour of legal decision making and provide a framework for professional debate in the context of the ways in which opposing views are determined.

Values and principles

Key aspects of the relationship between social work and law are the values and principles which shape the two professions. This is highlighted in the SCIE report as an area which is neglected by many social work degree programmes, and yet one which worries many social workers, despite the shared commitment of both professions to social justice. Critical analysis of how lawyers are governed and the principles which underpin their profession, including fairness, honesty, transparency, confidentiality and anti-discriminatory practice encourages students to see themselves as entitled to be regarded as equal players when in a professional role in court, and therefore in a unique position to make a difference to the experience of service users faced with court involvement. The General Social Care Council became the regulator of social care services in England (with companion organisations in Scotland, Wales and Northern Ireland) in October 2001 and produced the first codes of practice for social care workers and their employers in 2002 (GSCC, 2002). These codes describe the standards of professional conduct and practice required of social care workers, and also the responsibilities of social care employers. Whilst student social workers are learning to work in accordance with these codes and develop their understanding of the nature of professional relationships and boundaries, it is also helpful for them to consider service users' expectations of different professionals. This can be facilitated by means of structured exercises or reflections on personal experiences.

Observation and shadowing

Observation or shadowing can reduce anxiety by increasing knowledge of unfamiliar processes, but most importantly from a practice learning perspective, it is a means of developing self awareness and providing a framework for reflection.

> *The observational stance requires social workers to be aware of the environment, the verbal and non-verbal interaction; to be aware of their own responses as a source of invaluable data, provided that they are aware of what comes from them and what comes from their clients; and to develop the capacity to integrate these and give themselves time to think before arriving at a judgement or making a decision.*
>
> (Trowell and Miles, 1996, in Knott and Scragg, 2007, p 43)

Most courts, even those whose hearings are not open to the public, will permit people with a professional interest to attend a hearing, and many judges and magistrates are willing to have informal discussions afterwards, if approached through their clerk. Dickens (2005, 2006) has explored the tensions which can arise between local authority lawyers, social workers, and managers, and Brammer (2007, p 107) suggests that barriers to effective relationships between social workers and lawyers would be reduced by, among other things, the clarification of their respective roles and responsibilities. Students can be supported in developing their understanding of the legal/social work interface by being offered the opportunity to meet with and, if possible, shadow other professionals, for example in-house lawyers, children's guardians, and independent advocates, which is particularly beneficial if it occurs away from the tensions of actual proceedings. In addition to using supervision to encourage reflection on the opportunities and constraints of multidisciplinary working, practice assessors could devise a mini project as a framework for learning, such as preparation of an information leaflet for a particular client group on roles and responsibilities in legal proceedings.

Careful observation in the course of everyday activities will support the development of students' presentation skills, which are an important component of effective court work. Watching people presenting their views, or answering questions, in a variety of settings, such as television discussion programme, church service, lecture or party political broadcast, enables students to identify what seems to support effective communication and what creates barriers between speaker and listener.

Observation of interprofessional decision-making forums is also helpful, particularly if combined with an activity such as compiling a diagrammatic representation of group processes. It also helps students to understand the challenges of individual decision-making in the context of different cultures and priorities, and differing perceptions of professional duty, power, responsibility and autonomy.

Giving evidence

Students should be familiar with the concept of gathering evidence which relates to learning objectives, and the criteria put forward by Parker (2004, p 96) specifically to evidence practice learning, with the possible exception of the last element, can be transferred to the process of presenting evidence to court, thus further demonstrating that courtroom skills can be developed within a generic professional framework.

- Is it valid?

- Is it sufficient?

- Is it relevant?

- Is it based in social work values (and, I would add, codes of practice)?

- Is it reliable?

- Is it clear?

- Is it agreed?

Simple memory exercises, process recording or comparing different assessments of the same trigger will demonstrate the influence on evidence of shortcomings in memory and errors in perception, judgement or estimation and consequently the vital importance of comprehensive, accurate and fair recording.

Although courts need to know what professional opinions are being advanced, they are, if anything, more interested in how they were formed. In other words, what facts informed the analysis and how they were interpreted. Through their academic training, social work students should be developing an ability to move from description to the formulation of a rationale for their actions and opinions. This can be supported by practice assessors acting as 'devil's advocate' in suggesting alternative views, and encouraging students to incorporate four further Rs into the process.

- Reading (about relevant theories).

- Research (about 'what works').

- Resources (what are needed and, more importantly, are available to support any proposed plan).

- Reflection.

It is worth remembering that the best way to be a helpful witness is to understand the task facing the court, and so role plays (as in, for example, a planning or review meeting) can provide the opportunity to practise advancing, or defending, different professional judgements and opinions.

In relation to the sufficiency of evidence, an important aspect of court work is the need for social work evidence to include everything which might be relevant to the decision, even that which might be prejudicial to an individual's performance or the result they are hoping for. Also important in the context of collaborative and inter-disciplinary working is for students to learn to work with the fact that once in court, social workers are required to give evidence of their own knowledge and opinions, not those of anyone else. They do not have to support the line of the party on whose behalf they are giving evidence if, on professional grounds, they do not (Seymour and Seymour, 2007, pp 100–1). This is potentially difficult, since it requires professional confidence which usually only develops with experience. However, practice assessors can encourage students to question proposed courses of action, seek out and analyse alternatives in terms of the work they are doing, and also to identify and reflect upon things that, with hindsight, they might wish to do differently in the future. All of these activities will encourage the open-mindedness and fairness that courts, and also people who use social work services seek (ibid, p 73).

Report writing

In most situations in which social workers are involved professionally, their evidence will be presented to the court in writing, and consequently it is through their written work that their practice will, initially at least, be exposed to the scrutiny of others. Thus, reports and records are an important factor in determining the image of social work from the perspective of other professionals and potentially hold enormous power in the minds of service users.

There have been too many instances of social work reports to court failing to reach expected standards; specific criticisms have included lack of focus, failing to distinguish between fact and opinion, reproducing large sections of case records with little structure or editing, and, worst of all, failing to address the best interests of the child (Cooper, 2006, pp 1–2). Dickens (2004) found that a major complaint of local authority lawyers was the amount of time they had to spend on overseeing the quality of social workers' written statements. They were critical of standards of literacy, but their main concern was the proliferation of unnecessary detail and the inadequacy of analysis. Judges, too, cherish brevity and clarity (Bond and Sandhu, 2005) and reports which are poorly written or structured are likely to result in a negative opinion of the writer which is hard to reverse, however commendable their subsequent performance.

All of these areas can be addressed in the practice learning setting, by devising specific tasks, based on actual case records, which could include all, or some, of the following:

- compiling a genogram or chronology (neither of which should contain any opinion – a fact often overlooked);

- reducing large amounts of information without losing essential material or compromising fairness and balance;

- distinguishing between fact, analysis and opinion;

- expressing a rationale for opinions and decisions;

- presenting relevant theoretical and research material to support a rationale, including that which may not support the case being put forward;

- critical analysis of, and clarity in, use of language, including the identification and minimal use of jargon and acronyms.

Cross examination

As the aim of cross-examination is to expose any flaws in the evidence, it follows that evidence which has been properly prepared and presented by people who are familiar with their material, confident in their role and clear about the rationale for any opinions expressed, has the best chance of standing up to scrutiny. An effective cross-examiner is one who succeeds in obtaining from another party's witness evidence which assists their client's case, which means obtaining answers which the witness accepts are accurate, or at least more accurate than their previous evidence (Seymour and Seymour, 2007, p 113).

Although witnesses in the UK should never be coached on their actual evidence (unlike in the United States, where witness coaching is widely practised), preparation for the experience of being cross-examined can be facilitated by:

- compiling and maintaining records in such a way as to make them suitable to be shared with people who may have different interests in the case;

- anticipating the grounds on which evidence of fact might become subject to challenge (perception, memory, bias or prejudice, untruthfulness);

- anticipating the grounds on which evidence of opinion might be challenged (level or range of qualifications, experience or expertise, rationale);

- considering the influence of, and personal responses to, the crossexaminer's personal style;

- learning to recognise different types of question and their relationship to the sort of response sought;

- developing strategies to establish some control over the process, such as objectivity, controlling the pace, seeking clarification where necessary and keeping responses brief and focused.

The extensive transcripts of the Climbié Inquiry (**www.victoriaclimbié inquiry.org.uk**) provide a fascinating insight into the reality of cross-examination and are an invaluable learning resource for students.

After the hearing

At one level the justice system can be understood as the major institutional way we deal with losses, largely around our expectations of how other people will behave towards us.

(Dawes, in Thompson, 2002, p.176)

Any court experience is likely to involve loss for one or more of the people involved and this can provide a theoretical framework within which to plan responses in the aftermath of what could be distressing and damaging experiences. Potential losses range from those which are severe and permanent, such as the decision to place a child for adoption, to those from which recovery is possible and lessons can be learned, such as the restriction of liberty by means of a community sentence or having part, or all, of your evidence rejected by a court. For social workers, knowledge of models and theories of loss and of variations in the cultural needs of people experiencing loss can potentially make a significant difference to their own experiences and those of others who have been involved in the process. Supervision which actively encourages reflection and the application of relevant theories to practice will help students develop the confidence and independence of thought to question and critically analyse legal and court processes, which in turn will encourage them to see themselves as equal players in the court setting.

Conclusion

Social workers often describe their court experience as the most demanding of their career (Seymour and Seymour, 2007, p 151). Sometimes the experience is viewed negatively, but with effective preparation and support, it offers opportunities and challenges which do not arise in other areas of work. This article has sought to encourage practice assessors to help students build the foundations for developing the necessary knowledge and skills during the course of practice learning opportunities in which court work is undertaken.

Where the law meets social work, there may be a new mix of skills that brings together the principles and values of both professions and applies them to the task of developing lawful, ethical social work practice.

(SCIE, 2005, p 187)

References

Beckett, C, McKeigue, B and Taylor, H (2007) Coming to conclusions: social workers' perception of the decision-making process in care proceedings. *Child and Family Social Work,* 12(1): 54.

Bond, T and Sandhu, A (2005) *Therapists in court: providing evidence and supporting witnesses.* London: Sage.

Brammer, A (2007) *Social work law.* 2nd edn Harlow: Pearson Education.

Cooper, P (2006) *Reporting to the court under the Children Act.* 2nd edn London: Stationery Office.

Cull, L A and Roche, J (eds) (2001) *The law and social work.* Basingstoke: Palgrave.

Dickens, J (2004) Risks and responsibilities: the role of the local authority lawyer in childcare cases. *Child and Family Law Quarterly,* 16: 17.

Dickens, J (2005) The 'epitome of reason': the challenges for lawyers and social workers in care proceedings. *International Journal of Law, Policy and the Family,* 19: 73–101.

Dickens, J (2006) Care, control and change in childcare proceedings: dilemmas for social workers, managers and lawyers. *Child and Family Social Work,* 11(1): 23–32.

General Social Care Council (2002) *Code of practice for social care workers.* London: GSCC.

Knott, C and Scragg, T (eds) (2007) *Reflective practice in social work.* Exeter: Learning Matters.

Parker, J (2004) *Effective practice learning in social work.* Exeter: Learning Matters.

Preston-Shoot, M (2000) Making connections in the curriculum: law and professional practice, in Pierce, R and Weinstein, J (eds) *Innovative education and training for care professionals: a provider's guide.* London: Jessica Kingsley.

Quality Assurance Agency for Higher Education (QAA) (2000) *Social policy and administration and social work subject benchmark statements.* London: QAA

Seymour, C and Seymour, R (2007) *Courtroom skills for social workers.* Exeter: Learning Matters.

Social Care Institute for Excellence (SCIE) (2005) *Teaching, learning and assessment of law in social work education.* Bristol: Policy Press.

Thompson, N (ed) (2002) *Loss and grief.* Basingstoke: Palgrave.

FURTHER READING

Seymour, C and Seymour, R (2007) *Courtroom skills for social workers.* Exeter: Learning Matters.

Clare Seymour, Senior Lecturer in Social Work
Address for Correspondence: Anglia Ruskin University, Faculty of Health and Social Care, William Harvey Building, Bishop Hall Lane, Chelmsford CM1 1SQ.
c.v.seymour@anglia.ac.uk

Appendix 4

Using written skills: translating your learning from university to practice in developing case recording

Jonathan Parker and Angela Hickin

This appendix will help you to meet the following National Occupational Standards for Social Work.

- Key role 1,unit 1: prepare for social work contact and involvement.

- Key role 5, unit 16: manage, present and share records and reports.

Introduction

If you have just completed your social work qualification, whether at undergraduate or postgraduate level, you may have breathed a sigh of relief at having finished with writing academic assignments, essays, case studies and the written work associated with study. However, your use of the written word and the construction of reports, profiles, presentations and overviews has not ended, but it has changed and now, potentially as a newly qualified social worker, will have a significant bearing on the future of people with whom you are working.

Before reflecting gloomily on this prospect, the translation of writing skills from academe into practice is something that you can use effectively to advocate, record, argue, negotiate, and rely on, if it's done properly and viewed as an integral part of your role. If, on the other hand, it is seen as an additional burden and one that is not considered as important as directly working alongside people, you may find that a lack of attention to good written skills let you, your organisation and, most importantly, those who use your service, down. A recent review of serious case reviews highlights poor recording as a significant factor in contributing to poor outcomes for children. Poor recording can also lead to difficulties for reviewers when trying to piece together the 'story' of a case (Brandon *et al.*, 2008).

Writing skills and social work

It is worth considering for a moment the kinds of written work important for social work practice. The written word records work that has been undertaken, is being offered, and/or will be done. It is something that can be referred to, to justify, explain, and review actions. This is important not only as a means of protecting yourself and your agency if things were to go wrong, but as a means of improving on your practice by systematically reviewing what was done, what worked and why. You may think of your recording as a means of evaluating your work. Social workers operate in a wide variety of roles and fields and some written tasks will be more appropriate in some areas than others. However, it is likely that you will be involved in constructing some of the following in the course of your work:

- case recording (including key information sheets, contact records, closure summaries);
- chronologies and case histories;
- referral documents;
- assessment reports;
- intervention reports;
- case reviews and evaluations;
- court reports and conference reports;
- communication and letters/emails (with people who use services and carers, other professionals and internally).

Case recording

If we focus on case recording as a central skill and task, we note a problematic history. In 1999, Goldsmith (1999) prepared a report for the Department of Health aimed at improving case recording in then social services departments. Inspections of case recording demonstrated a lack of attention to case records. Unfortunately, case recording was one element of the inquiry into the death of Victoria Climbié that was noted as seriously inadequate (Laming, 2003; see 7.28–7.30).

Recognising the shortfall in practice, the Department of Health commissioned the development of a set of training materials to respond to these inadequacies (Walker *et al.*, 2005), by offering interactive exercises and drawing together messages from research, inspections and inquiry reports relating to children's services – even though the basic principles are shared across all social work areas. This set of training materials put centre stage the importance of case recording as a means of improving the quality of practice. If we look at the current Cafcass (2008) case recording policy we can see how the lessons from past inadequacies are being applied to current social work practice. This document sets out the reasons for case recording, legislation issues and the particular practice associated with it at Cafcass (2008). It also considers issues of quality – you will hopefully be familiar with these from your qualifying social work programme.

- Case recordings should be of high quality: structured, analytical and proportionate to the requirements of the case.

- Case records should be legible. Legibility will be examined during any monitoring process – in the same way as your work would be for an essay or exam.

- Ethical principles need to be identified – facts need to be distinguished from opinions – and respect for carers and people who use services is central.

- Reflection and analysis can also be included.

Often your employing agency will have guidance on record keeping or case recording, for example see Plymouth City Council's documentation: **www.plymouth.gov.uk/record-keeping** (accessed 2 February 2009) in this case for work in foster care. If you have recently joined a team, search out the case recording policy – increasingly these are on the web, but it will be written down if not – and familiarise yourself with it. It is sometimes worth comparing the policy of your agency with one or two others. This will give you a good idea of the common features; those core elements of recording that are necessary wherever you work and in whatever field you practise.

ACTIVITY **A4.1**

Writing for practice

Reflection point
Think back to your social work qualification, the written work you undertook on placement and the notes made for essays and other assignments.

- What skills can you use from your social work education to enhance the quality of your written work?

- *What's similar or different and why?*

- *How can you allocate time and energy in an efficient and effective way that recognises the importance of the task and its skilled completion?*

In answering the question, '*What skills can you transfer from your social work education?*', you may have identified some of the following core elements:

Planning	Consider carefully the purposes of what you are about to write and who you are writing it for. Set out what to include, how to gather any information and how to complete the process.
Structure	Make sure your work is organised and focused, introduces the issues, debates them and offers a clear and logical analysis.
Presentation	Be careful to maximise the immediate visual impact of your document. Proofread it carefully to identify 'typos' and sentences that are not as clear as they could be and to ensure its readability and accessibility.

Evidenced and sourced	Ensure that fact and opinion are distinguished and that the source of evidence for any statements, conclusions, recommendations, etc., is clear and accessible.
Logical argument and analysis	Develop a style that weighs up and evaluates arguments and alternatives and one that is balanced and based upon knowledge and research evidence where appropriate.
Theoretical	Analysis and evidence should be theoretically informed to enable a conclusion to be drawn.
Timeliness	Ensure that reports are lodged with relevant bodies (funding, other agencies, courts) in good time, making sure that case records are up-to-date and completed as near to the event as possible, and that communication with others is timely.

These are, no doubt, elements you came across when undertaking your qualifying programme. They indicate that the consolidation of your learning and transfer of your skills and competences (meta-learning) is key now that you are qualified. It is not, as more cynical workers may suggest, time to leave behind your education but instead to hone and develop its use for working alongside and with people to effect change, make a difference and safeguard.

In many situations, case records will be used to inform decisions made in relation to the allocation of limited resources. It is therefore important to ensure that reports are concise, factual, evidence-based, and with analysis of the situation that is reflective of needs. This will enable readers to make an informed decision about the case and will help an appropriate allocation of resources.

The following case study shows how important the transfer of learning about record keeping can be.

CASE STUDY A4.1

A short case study

A case was recently presented to a panel for decision in relation to a request to accommodate a young person. The young person, James, has autism accompanied by severe learning disabilities and challenging behaviour. The behaviour included threatening behaviour towards his parents and siblings (including holding a knife to his mother's throat), inability to sleep for longer than three hours, tantrums, switching lights on throughout the night, screaming and so forth. He is also incontinent and requires constant supervision and, during tantrums, two-to-one care.

In order to make an informed decision in relation to this case, the social worker presented the panel with a report that initially described James' behaviour, placing it in the context of his home, school and residential respite unit. She described how his autism impacted on his ability to understand his actions and interpret the behaviour of others. She used evidence from her experience and the experience of others, and clearly stated her opinion of the situation based on factual evidence.

She described in her report the impact that this behaviour was having on each member of the family and the effect this had on the family to function as a 'system', for example the mother's inability to perform her role as mother to James' siblings due to his high level of need. Her arguments were theoretically based, helping to clearly set out all the relevant information in a concise, understandable and readable way.

She then went on to analyse the information – for example, looking not just at 'what' behaviour James displayed in which setting but 'why'. She analysed the reasons why James' behaviour was more manageable in the structured environment of a residential respite unit than in the home, and how the stresses of coping were impacting on the family. She explained and analysed the risk factors of the situation versus the protective factors of the situation and how these impacted on the family's ability to cope with James.

Along with a comprehensive discussion of previous interventions and support offered to the family the social worker was clearly able to identify that this was a family that had been in severe difficulty for some time and to detail James' needs in terms of the need for stability, consistency and attachment. She was also able to clearly state the needs of the family to access support and therapy in order to help them continue to care for James in the future. This enabled the panel to make a decision to accommodate James, with a view to achieving the outcome of his eventual return home.

The panel were also able to identify that, had intensive behavioural support been offered earlier, James may not have needed to be accommodated in order to safeguard and promote his welfare, and may well have been able to remain for longer within the family home.

So, we can see that high quality written work is central to good social work practice. It will be helpful briefly to identify what are the valuable aspects of written work. The principles for case recording identified by Cafcass (2008) provide a clear agency perspective on key elements constituting written work. These include writing only what needs to be recorded and not duplicating material where possible (*proportionality*), writing in accordance with the law, especially the Data Protection Act 1998 (*accountability*) and ensuring records are shared with people who use services wherever possible (*transparency*). Case records and files should be *accessible* and kept *safe*. It is useful to add the following key points important to case recording.

- Ensure that you write in a clear, simple and accessible style free from jargon and ensuring that any specific and technical/professional language is explained in plain English.

- Write in a concrete and behavioural way that distinguishes between fact and opinion.

- Make sure you set out the evidence base you have used, and where the information can be consulted if appropriate. In some reports it will help your case if you use appropriate references and source material. It allows your work to be subject to challenge and scrutiny and this is only fair when dealing with sensitive situations and potentially vulnerable people. If a case goes to court, the court will expect that you have based your arguments within a theoretical framework, so it is important to be clear about *why* you have reached a particular conclusion.

- Like the skills transferred from your education, organise and structure written work in a way that sets things out in a logical order and sequence.

In summary

In this short piece we have focused predominantly on case recording. However, what we have discussed applies equally to the development of informative literature, media advertising the services your agency offers, funding bids for your agency, and more formal report writing. High quality writing skills will assist you in providing the best possible service to people with whom you are working.

FURTHER READING

In addition to the references cited, you may wish to follow up your reading and to consult the following.

Brown, K and Rutter, L (2008) *Critical thinking for social work*, 2nd edn Exeter: Learning Matters.

In particular, look at Chapter 5, which is about reflective academic writing.

Healy, K and Mulholland, J (2007) *Writing skills for social workers*. London: Sage.

This book aims to raise the profile of writing skills in social work practice, and to enhance social workers' written communication skills.

Northern Ireland Government – Department for Health, Social Services and Public Safety. Available from: **www.dhsspsni.gov.uk/safeguard_chpt8.pdf** (accessed 2 February 2009)

This is a useful and well-written chapter on record keeping, confidentiality and sharing information.

Parker, J (2004) *Effective practice learning in social work*. Exeter: Learning Matters.

In particular, please refer to Chapter 6, developing skills and communicating effectively.

Walker, S, Shemmings, D and Cleaver, H (2005) *Write enough: interactive training materials to support quality recording in children's social services*, **www.writeenough.org.uk** (accessed 2 February 2009).

Commissioned by the Department of Health to support quality recording via interactive exercises based on messages from research, inspections and inquiry reports.

Appendix 5

Child protection for newly qualified social workers

Jill Davey and Richard Williams

Child Protection is a complex matter. To work alongside families with such issues requires a considerable amount of skill and judgement. The impact of high profile cases, such as Victoria Climbié and more recently Baby P, make entry into the specialism of Child Protection a matter for serious consideration. In theory, the overwhelmingly negative media portrayal of social workers should deter the most enthusiastic social work student and steer them speedily away from working with children and families. Yet, there is something about working with children/young people and their respective families/carers that can provide the most challenging and rewarding of experiences. For what the media forgets, or fails to portray, is what a privilege it is to work with such families and the personal knowledge that by supporting them you can have a positive and significant impact in their lives.

To look at child protection in any detail, would certainly take more than the space we are permitted within this book and therefore we can only hope to give you some sign posts for those starting out in this worthwhile area of practice. Remember, you don't have to be a childcare practitioner to become involved in child protection matters, safeguarding is a priority for every social worker. At the end of this Appendix we have highlighted key reading related to safeguarding children.

Know the policy and procedures

Whatever organisation you work within, you have to know your own organisation's Child Protection Policies and Procedures. Every one of us has a responsibility towards the protection of children. It is essential for you to know how to refer such matters and to whom to refer them, at the very start of your employment.

Use supervision well

The unique opportunities we have as social workers to receive supervision should be received with enthusiasm and viewed as such – Chapter 3 should be especially helpful to you in this regard. Asking for advice, assistance or support should never be seen as a weakness, but as strength and a way of evidencing your desire to grow as a practitioner. It is essential you use this opportunity to explore both the professional and personal impact of child protection work. As Chapter 4 reminds you, the need to critically reflect on your practice is not something just for the newly qualified social worker, but is an ongoing process throughout your career. Use supervision effectively by being open and honest about how you are managing.

Joint working – learning from the multidisciplinary team

Shadowing and joint working opportunities are essential for newly qualified social workers and allow you to observe experienced practitioners at work. This will allow you to become familiar with procedures and policies and to see the skilled practitioners communicating with families, empowering families, and assessing risk. You do not just have to rely on your immediate colleagues to gain experience; colleagues from other professions all contribute to the protection of children. Chapter 6 is a useful section of this handbook as it is all about joining and contributing to a team.

The Child Protection Conference and Child Protection Register (CPR)

The CPR is the register of children and young people for whom a multi-disciplinary child protection conference has decided there are significant child protection risks and on whose behalf a child protection plan has been devised; the implementation of this plan is co-ordinated by the social worker with case responsibility for the child/young person. All agencies must work together to support the child and their family and thereby address any issues of concern.

Child Protection Orders and Police powers

The legal duties and powers with regard to child protection are, as you know, extensive and complex. You will need to retain up to date knowledge of these and you may find the following publication a practical resource.

Davis, L (2008) *The social worker's guide to children and families law*. London: Jessica Kingsley.

Recognising and managing risk

The recognition and management of risk is a fundamental part of being a social worker, whatever specialism you choose. For child protection social workers it has to be at the forefront of your decision making processes. The recognition of risk is often drawn out through the assessment process and the enquiring nature of the social worker. Making decisions regarding child protection issues is not the responsibility of any one social worker, newly qualified or not. Child protection is a joint responsibility both within your organisation and on a multi-professional basis. It is therefore essential that you become familiar with the structure of your organisation, with whom you discuss such issues and the availability of relevant staff. Discussing such matters anywhere other than within the professional arena is a serious breach of confidentiality. The process of assessment has been developed to respond to needs early and thereby work pro-actively to prevent crises happening – the first of these Appendices is all about assessment. The Common Assessment Framework is the generic tool to assess the needs of children and young people using an ecological approach. The link below takes you to this assessment tool. **www.everychildmatters.gov.uk/deliveringservices/caf/** (accessed 24 March 2009).

Confidentiality

Issues of confidentiality are often seen as confusing. Professionals are aware of the tensions that may occur between sharing information that may breach the Data Protection Act 1998 and the need to uphold someone's human rights. However, when it comes to child protection we must be clear – we must share information of which we become aware. We must share concerns via the appropriate procedures. Never 'hold back' information because it would be easier to do so, or because you have been asked to do so by a person who uses services. If you believe the information is relevant and of a serious nature it should be referred immediately to the appropriate person and always recorded in your records, including the outcome of your referral.

Record keeping

Finally, although the previous Appendix (4) has already touched on writing skills, it is essential that you follow your employer's guidance on record keeping. Not only should you record contact with people who use services but also your decision making processes. Anyone, who has authorisation to access the file, should be able to see how the case is progressing, the decision making process and the relevant supervision notes. Remember the case recordings should accurately reflect your work and input into the case. The Code of Practice (GSCC, 2004) clearly lays out the standards expected of you as a social worker and that of your employers. You have responsibilities to each other and it is an essential document that should be used as a working tool.

FURTHER READING

Calder, M (2008) *Contemporary risk assessment in safeguarding children.* Lyme Regis: Russell House.

Risk and risk assessment are key considerations and preoccupations when safeguarding children. This tome provides varied and illuminating perspectives that will help refine your professional judgement.

There are also a number of useful publications you may wish to refer to from the old Department for Education and Skills. These include:

DfES (2003) *Every child matters.* London: DfES.

DfES (2006) *Working together to safeguard children: a guide for interagency working to safeguard and promote the welfare of children.* London: TSO.

DfES (2006a) *What to do if you are worried a child is being abused.* London: DfES.

Appendix 6

Working towards consolidation of practice: advice from a PQ lecturer

Melanie Forsyth Smith

What follows is a summary of the hints and tips I have amassed over several years of supporting) over 1700 PQ (post-qualifying) students who have risen to the challenge of consolidating their practice – mostly, I must say, with the humour, goodwill and optimism that I believe epitomise the unique qualities of our profession. The four main topic areas of this appendix (reflective writing; what and how to write; theory and critical reflection) will, I hope, support you through the demands of your first likely step into the world of professional development – the consolidation programme.

In my experience, most view PQ education as a positive development opportunity. Indeed by the time you read this PQ may have been made compulsory. Although some may view it as yet another imposed and demanding hurdle to jump in order to remain credible, or even employed, I believe that any profession worth being committed to should make demands of its practitioners to continually prove themselves; to challenge, reflect on and develop their practice.

Any education programme worth its salt makes demands on students, especially those engaged in 'work based learning'. Newly qualified social workers are not, after all, like most average students, responsible only for meeting the demands of their academic programme. However, the consolidation of practice is a developmental process in its own right, and not just the gateway to the specialist award. It provides you with an opportunity to develop skills that will significantly enhance, not just further professional training experiences but day-to-day professional practice. These skills tend to be undervalued in the process and procedure driven world of everyday practice, but hopefully you will quickly recognise their significance and value – it is to reflective writing I turn first.

Reflective writing

Writing about practice and for practice are not unfamiliar skills for social work practitioners, but the term 'reflective writing' introduces another skill level. As Jenny Moon (2005) acknowledges, reflective writing is a developmental exercise, enabling the writer to literally take another look at practice, using the processes involved in transferring thoughts to paper, to clarify, decipher and gain a deeper understanding.

Reflective writing refers to the processes involved in writing that can be utilised as means in themselves to help us learn from our experiences (Rolfe *et al.*, 2001, p 42). Therefore the writing of reflective assignments for PQ programmes is not just a means for assessment, but also an opportunity to learn. The Consolidation and Preparation for Specialist Practice Unit may be the first opportunity for you to write reflectively about your practice, and this production of a paper version of your thoughts provides a chance for review (Moon, 2005). For this reason I encourage consolidation students to jot down the ideas they wish to discuss as they begin to analyse practice in relation to programme requirements – my mantra being *get something down on paper*. These jottings help the student to begin the exploration process, deciding what is important enough to be written down, identifying themes, choosing the areas for deeper thought, beginning analyses and organising the often overwhelming amount of potential material that most students find when they start to think reflectively about practice. It is a process where 'writing most clearly interacts with thinking and learning' (Moon, 2005, p 13). So, reflective writing reflects and supports the development of skills in critical reflection; more of which later. Now I turn to what to write and how to write it.

What to write – and how to write it

Assignments within the Consolidation and Preparation for Specialist Practice (often known as CPSP) portfolio, and indeed all the specialist awards, mostly require the student to write in the first person. This is, of course, not the norm for academic assignments, but is relevant, in my opinion essential, for demonstrating the self awareness, analysis and critique required in writing reflectively about practice (Brown and Rutter, 2008).

Exemplars from successful PQ portfolios (normally provided with programme documentation) will show that there are different styles of reflective academic writing, each one personal to the author. Your own style will develop as you practise. Personally, I prefer a writing style that allows me to grasp the meaning of the sentence upon first read – preferably without the use of a dictionary. Academic-speak has its place, of course, but for the PQ student, the advice is to keep it simple, keep it focused, and state the obvious. Identify early on what you are going to write about, and, equally importantly, what you are going to leave out. An analysis of practice, the type of assignment often required within a PQ programme, is not a 'case study'. Instead, the focus is on providing a detailed examination of an example of your professional practice, rather than writing a more superficial overview of many events. As Fook and Askeland (2007, p 521) observe these examples are normally 'critical incidents'; a specific and concrete example of some piece of practice which was significant for the participant. The bulk of the account should consist of the in depth examination of why and how you did what you did, your recognition of the influences and constraints upon your actions, and an evaluation of your practice and its outcome. But where does theory fit in?

Theory? What theory?

The skills and knowledge base used, incorporating methods, models, legislation, policy, theory, research, values, and professional ethics, should automatically be identified through the reflective process described above. It still surprises me how often I am met by an uncomfortable silence in practitioners confronted by the requirement to link theory to practice – a requirement that although running explicitly through the social work education framework, is still often met with an attitude I call the *'Theory? What theory?'* approach.

This reaction is understandable in as much as the theory base for social work is extraordinarily wide. No one theory, method, model, paradigm, perspective or approach 'fits all' in social work practice – or even comes close, as we have to make sense of 'multiple perspectives gathered from a range of different sources' (Paterson, 2002 in Trevithick, 2005, p 23). This is why as a profession we draw on many areas of knowledge from a variety of disciplines, particularly those that align with our own professional value base. But although we use theory as a starting point, we adapt and develop our ideas in response to changing scenarios. This type of learning tends to be known as practice wisdom (Trevithick, 2005) or, when more intuitive, tacit knowledge (Gabbay and le May, 2004) is related to the 'knowledge gained from watching what colleagues do, trial and error, reflective practice, peer approval, client satisfaction and so on' (Pawson *et al.*, 2003, p 11). Perhaps it should not be surprising then that most practitioners find that 'much of this experiential knowledge and theory-in-use is extremely difficult to articulate' (Rolfe *et al.*, 2001, p 12) and to do so requires us to stand back from our practice and reflect on it at a deeper level, asking – why did I do that? and how did I know that? – to identify our own personal knowledge base.

When explaining your use of knowledge, please do not leave the reader to make the links between what you have done and why you have done it – for instance, if you have chosen a certain method of assessment, communication or intervention because it is more empowering, respectful or more likely to enable the client to have their thoughts and wishes heard, then say so. Where you have recognised that you did some particularly good value-based work, used strong and well developed skills or extended your knowledge of theory or research – again, please say so. There is no place for subtlety in reflective writing. Now I return to critical reflection, the final topic area.

Critical reflection

Critical reflection can be seen as a challenging and time consuming activity that is not often facilitated within normal working environments; the workplace appears to be becoming more and more procedure and regulation based (Fook and Askeland, 2007), demanding that students must be ready for, not critical of, practice (Preston-Shoot, 2000, p 88). This helps to explain why I often find that PQ students approach reflective writing, and its demand for critical reflection and self evaluation, with trepidation. Critical reflection, to any useful depth, requires time and space which is not normally available to the busy practitioner – nor is it often encouraged. A sense of confusion about what critical reflection means is also not uncommon as there appear to be as many interpretations of the term as there are books about it. You may not be helped either by the terms used by the GSCC (2005a) in its requirements – for instance, you must:

- critically evaluate the effectiveness of your practice;
- critically review knowledge and theoretical frameworks; and
- use reflection and analysis to think critically about your practice.

148

Perhaps more helpful interpretations are:

- working through for oneself, afresh, a problem (Kneale, 2003, p 3);

- weighing up the arguments for and against (Cottrell, 1999, p 188);

- a sustained and systematic process of examination (Moon, 2005, p 5).

These readily make sense when applied to reflecting on practice situations. However, the capacity for critical thinking is a developmental process in itself (Moon, 2005). So, the consolidation programme can enable first steps in this direction. Although there are many models of critical reflection encouraging the questioning of practice to differing levels of analysis (e.g. Johns,1998), I encourage students to initially adapt one model that works for them, within their own context of practice experience. You can use the questions laid out of Figures 4.1.and 4.2 of Chapter 4 – or you can use other simple questions such as:

- What did you do?

- Why did you do it?

- How did you do it?

- How did it go?

They encourage an examination of practice rather than events, encouraging you to explain and evaluate your actions and decisions. This entails self evaluation; words that I find can elicit a state of nervous silence from even the most efficient and competent practitioner, yet to evaluate the effectiveness of [your] practice (GSCC 2005a) is one of the essential requirements of PQ education.

Practitioners can often appear reticent to acknowledge their competence. In my view, this is partly due to an organisational culture of professional evaluation that only responds publicly after high profile media cases, and which otherwise lives quietly with widespread misunderstanding and misinterpretation of what social workers are and do. This has led to a profession that evaluates defensively rather than positively. As a result we can be slow to acknowledge our own strengths and skills. A practitioner's skill base develops gradually and because many skills are involved in even the most simple processes, these often become second nature – intuitive – and can go unnoticed. Trevithick (2005, see pages 81–82 and page 124) outlines 20 skills relating to the seemingly routine task of interviewing along with seven practice approaches and 50 generic skills that reflect the baseline expectations of competence in almost any practice situation. Revisiting such textbooks will help the process of identifying skills that have become intuitive. Discussion with colleagues can also help this process. Most consolidation programmes require a 'third party' testimony, which will involve others in a positive evaluation process to highlight your strengths.

In summary

Through my teaching on PQ programmes, I have become aware that the vast majority of social work practice is of a very high standard indeed. I talk here both from the experience of marking consolidation portfolios, and from external examiners' reports attached to the programmes I run. These evidence the very high quality of work that is going on, day-to-day, quietly and efficiently, by practitioners in a variety of agencies, providing an excellent service to a huge number and variety of individuals in need. There are few occasions when social workers are thanked or congratulated on a job well done. I sincerely hope as a newly qualified practitioner that you too are able to recognise the value of the consolidation programme as a process through which your professional competence can gain recognition, as well as it being a challenging, satisfying, developmental experience.

FURTHER READING

Brown, K and Rutter, L (2008) *Critical thinking for social work.* 2nd edn Exeter: Learning Matters.

This provides not only a very readable overview of the practical application of thinking skills, but also excellent guidance on writing reflective academic assignments.

Rolfe, G, Freshwater, D and Jasper, M (2001) *Critical reflection for nursing.* Hants: Palgrave.

Rolfe *et al.* (2001) provide an excellent discussion of how to develop critical reflection and, in particular, reflective writing skills, through models, methods and reflective writing exercises.

References

Adams, R (2005) Working within and across boundaries: tensions and dilemmas, in Adams, R Payne, M and Dominelli L (eds) *Social work future.* Basingstoke: Routledge, pp 99–114.

Adams, R, Dominelli, L and Payne, M (2002a) *Social work – themes, issues and critical debates.* Basingstoke: Palgrave.

Adams, J D, Hayes, J, and Hopson, B (1976) *Transition: understanding and managing personal change.* London: Martin Robertson.

Argyris, C and Schön, D (1978) *Organizational learning: a theory of action perspective.* Reading, MA: Addison Wesley.

Argyris, C and Schön, D (1974) *Theory in practice: increasing professional effectiveness.* San Francisco: Jossey-Bass.

Barr, H, Goosey, D and Webb, M (2008) Social work in collaboration with other professions, in Davies, M (ed) *The Blackwell companion to social work.* 3rd edn Oxford: Blackwell, pp 277–86.

Bates, N, Immins, T, Parker, Keen, S, Rutter, L, Brown, K, Zsigo, S (2009) Baptism of fire: the first year in the life of a newly qualified social worker. *Social Work Education.* In press.

Beresford, P (2003) *It's our lives: a short theory of knowledge, distance and experience.* London: Citizen Press.

Beresford, P (2007) *The changing roles and tasks of social work: from service user perspectives – a literature informed discussion paper.* London: Shaping Our Lives.

Blair, S E E (2000) The centrality of occupation during life transitions. *British Journal of Occupational Therapy,* 63: 231–7.

Blewitt, J and Tunstall, J (2008) *Fit for purpose? The Social Work Degree in 2008.* London: GSCC.

Borrill, C, West, M, Carter, M, and Dawson, J (2003) The relationship between staff satisfaction and patient satisfaction, Research paper. Aston: Aston Business School

Bostock, L, Bairstow, S, Fish, S and Macleod, F (2005) *Managing risk and minimising mistakes in services to children and families.* London: SCIE. Available from: **www.scie.org.uk/publications/reports/report06.asp** (accessed 31 March 2009).

Bradley, G (2006) *Using research findings to change agency culture and practice. Research Policy and Planning,* 24(3): 135–48.

Brandon, M, Belderson, P, Warren, C, Howe, Gardner, R, Dodsworth, J and Black, J (2008) *Analysing child deaths and serious injury through abuse and neglect: what can we learn? A biennial analysis of serious case reviews 2003–2005.* London: DCSF. Available from: **www.dcsf.gov.uk/research/data/uploadfiles/dcsf-RB023.pdf** (accessed 26 March 2009).

Brechin, A, Brown, H and Eby, M (eds) (2000) *Critical practice in health and social care*, London: Sage.

Brown, K and Keen, S (2004) Post Qualifying Awards in Social Work (Part 1): necessary evil or panacea? *Social Work Education* 23(1): 77–92.

Brown, K, Keen, S and Rutter, L (2006) *Partnerships, CPD and APL.* Birmingham: Learn to Care.

Brown, K and Rutter, L (2006) *Critical thinking for social work.* 1st edn Exeter: Learning Matters.

Brown, K and Rutter, L (2008) *Critical thinking for social work.* 2nd edn Exeter: Learning Matters.

Brown, K, Immins, T, Bates, N, Gray, I, Rutter, L, Keen, S, Parker, J and members of the Project's Steering Group (2007) *Tracking the learning and development needs of newly qualified social workers project.* Bournemouth: Bournemouth University.

Brown, L, Tucker, C, and Domokos, T (2003) Evaluating the impact of integrated health and social care teams on older people living In the community. *Health and Social Care in the Community*, 11: 85–94.

Brumfitt, S, Enderby, P M, and Hoben, K (2005) The transition to work of newly qualified speech and language therapists: implications for the curriculum. *Learning in Health and Social Care*, 4: 142–55.

Cafcass (2008) CAFCASS Case Recording Policy. Available from: **www.cafcass.gov.uk/idoc.ashx?docid=ebc3bff0-1d0d-4fee-9ce3-6a0d1eefa7bb&version=-1** (accessed 2 February 2009).

Calder, M (2008) Contemporary risk assessment in safeguarding children. Lyme Regis: Russell House.

Calder, M and Hackett, S (2003) *Assessment in childcare: using and developing frameworks for practice.* Lyme Regis: Russell House Publishing.

Cameron, C (2003) Care work and care workers, in *Social care workforce research: needs and priorities.* Kings College, London: Social Care Workforce Research Unit.

Carpenter, J (2005) *Evaluating outcomes in social work education.* Dundee: Social Care Institute for Excellence/Scottish Institute for Excellence in Social Work Education.

CEC (Commission of the European Communities) (2007) *Action plan on adult learning. It's always a good time to learn.* Brussels: Commission of the European Communities. Available from: **http://ec.europa.eu/education/policies/adult/com558_en.pdf** (accessed 20 August 2008).

Centre for Human Services Technology (undated) *What is research mindedness.* Available from: **www.resmind.swap.ac.uk/content/02_what_is/what_is_02.htm** (accessed 26 March 2009).

Charles, M and Butler, S (2004) Management of organisational change, in Lymbery, M and Butler, S (eds) *Social work ideals and practice realities.* Basingstoke: Palgrave, pp 40–50.

Collins, S (2007) Resilience, positive emotion and optimism. *Practice*, 19(4): 255–70.

Collins, S (2008) Statutory social workers: Stress, job satisfaction, coping, social support and individual differences. *British Journal of Social Work*, 39: 1173–93.

Cottrell, S (1999) *The study skills handbook.* Basingstoke: Macmillan.

Cooper, B and Rixon, A (2001) Integrating post-qualification study into the workplace: the candidates' experience. *Social Work Education*, 20: 701–16.

Coulshed, V and Orme, J (2006) *Social work practice: an introduction.* 4th edn Basingstoke: Palgrave.

Covey, S (1989) *The 7 habits of highly effective people.* New York: Simon Schuster.

Cree, V (ed) (2003) *Becoming a social worker.* London: Routledge.

Crisp, B, Anderson, M, Orme, J and Lister, (2003) Knowledge Review 1. *Learning and teaching in social work education. Assessment.* London: Social care Institute for Excellence (SCIE).

Cunningham, J and Cunningham, S (2008) *Sociology and social work.* Exeter: Learning Matters.

CWDC (2008) *Newly qualified social worker pilot programme 2008–2011. Outcome statements and guidance.* Leeds: CWDC.

CWDC (2008a) *CWDC Social Work Projects. Annexe B and C.* Leeds: CWDC.

Davis, L (2008) The social worker's guide to children and families law. London: Jessica Kingsley.

DCSF (2006) Every child matters. Change for children – multi-agency services: advice on managing change. Available from: **www.everychildmatters.gov.uk/deliveringservices/ multiagencyworking/managerstoolkit/managingchange/advice/** (accessed 17 February 2009).

DfES (2003) *Every child matters.* London: DfES.

DfES (2006) *Working together to safeguard children: a guide for interagency working to safeguard and promote the welfare of children.* London: TSO.

DfES (2006a) *What to do if you are worried a child is being abused.* London: DfES.

DfES/DH (Department of Health), (2006). *Options for excellence: building the social care workforce of the future.* London: DfES/DH.

DH (Department of Health) (1998) *Modernising social services.* London: TSO.

DH (2000) *The framework for the assessment of children in need and their families.* London: TSO. Available from: **www.dh.gov.uk/en/publicationsandstatistics/publications/publications policyandguidance/dh_4008144** (accessed 29 January 2009).

DH (Department of Health) (2002) *Requirements for social work training.* London: HMSO.

DH (2005) Mental Capacity Act. London: TSO.

DH (2006) *Reward and recognition.* London: DH. Available from: **www.dh.gov.uk/en/ publicationsandstatistics/publications/publicationspolicyandguidance/dh_4138523** (accessed 18 February 2009).

DH (2007). *Putting people first: a shared vision and commitment to the transformation of adult social care.* Available from: **www.dh.gov.uk/en/publicationsandstatistics/ publications/publicationspolicyandguidance/dh_081118** (accessed 20 March 2009).

DH (2008) *Carers at the heart of 21st century communities: a caring system on your side, a life of your own.* Available from: **www.dh.gov.uk/en/publicationsandstatistics/publicationspolicyandguidance/ DH_085345** (accessed 19 May 2009).

DH (2009) *Working to put people first: the strategy for the adult social care workforce in England.* Available from **www.dh.gov.uk/en/publicationsandstatistics/publications/ publicationspolicyandguidance/DH_09848** (accessed 19 May 2009).

Dilts, R and DeLozier, J (2000) Encyclopaedia of Systemic NLP and NLP New Coding. Available from: **www.//nlpuniversitypress.com/** (accessed 26 March 2009).

Doel, M, Flynn and E, Nelson, P (2006*) Experiences of post-qualifying study in social work.* Leeds: Skills for Care.

Doel, M, Flynn, E and Nelson, P (2008) Experiences of post qualifying study in social work. *Social Work Education,* 27(5): 549–71.

Dominelli, L (2005) Social work research: contested knowledge for practice, in Adams, R, Dominelli, L and Payne, M (eds) *Social work futures: crossing boundaries, transforming practice.* Basingstoke: Palgrave, pp 223–36.

ESWDQET (Evaluation of Social Work Degree Qualification in England Team) (2008) *Evaluation of the new social work degree qualification in England. Volume 1: findings.* London: King's College Social Care Workforce Research Unit.

Everitt, A and Hardiker, P (1996) *Evaluating for good practice.* Basingstoke: BASW/Macmillan.

Fish, S, Munro, E, Bairstow, S (2008) *SCIE guide 24: leading together to safeguard children: developing a multi-agency systems approach to case reviews.* London:SCIE. Available from: **www.scie.org.uk/publications/guides/guide24/index.asp** (accessed 19 February 2009).

Fook, J and Askeland, G A (2007) Challenges of critical reflection: nothing ventured, nothing gained. *Social Work Education,* 26 (5): 520–33.

Fouad, N A and Bynner, J (2008) Work transitions. *American Psychologist,* May–June: 241–251.

Fowler, A (1996) E*mployee induction – a good start.* London: IPD.

Gabbay, J and le May, A (2004) Evidence based guidelines or collectively conducted 'mindlines?' Ethnographic study of knowledge management in primary care. *British Medical Journal,* 329: 1013–6.

Galpin, D (2009) Who really drives the development of Post-Qualifying Social Work Education and what are the implications of this? *Social Work Education,* 26: 65–80.

Gauntlett, A N (2005) Evaluation of a postgraduate training programme for community mental health practitioners. *Journal of Psychiatric and Mental Health Nursing,* 12: 223–30.

Gendlin, E (1996) Focussing oriented psychotherapy: a manual of the experiential method. New York: Guilford Press.

Gerrish, K (2000) Still fumbling along? A comparative study of the newly qualified nurse's perception of the transition from student to qualified nurse. *Journal of Advanced Nursing*, 32: 473–480.

Gibson, F, McGrath, A and Reid, N (1989) Occupational stress in social work. *British Journal of Social Work*, 19: 1–16.

Gilligan, P (2007) Well motivated reformists or nascent radicals: how do applicants to the degree in social work see social problems, their origins and solutions. *British Journal of Social Work*, 37: 735–60.

Goldsmith, L (1999) *Recording with care: inspection of case recording in social services department. London: DH.* Available from: **www.dh.gov.uk/en/publicationsandstatistics/ publications/publicationspolicyandguidance/DH_4010129** (accessed 2 February 2009).

Goleman, D (1996) *Emotional intelligence.* London: Bloomsbury.

Gould, N and Baldwin, M (2004) (eds) *Social work, critical reflection and the learning organization.* Aldershot: Ashgate.

GSCC (2004) *Code of practice for social care workers.* London: GSCC. Available from: **www.gscc.org.uk/nr/rdonlyres/8E693C62-9B17-48E1-A806-3F6F280354FD/0/codesof practice.doc** (accessed 17 February 2009).

GSCC (2005a) *Post-qualifying framework for social work education and training.* London: GSCC.

GSCC (2005b) *Post registration training and learning (PRTL) requirements for registered social workers. Advice and guidance on good practice.* London: GSCC.

Hamm, R M (1988) Clinical intuition and clinical analysis; expertise and the cognitive continuum, in Dowie, J A and Elstein, A S (eds) *Professional judgement; a reader in clinical decision making.* Cambridge: Cambridge University Press, pp 78–105.

Handy, C (1993) *Understanding organisations.* 4th ed. London: Penguin.

Hansard (2007) *House of Lord Debates.* 8 October, column 88–94.

Harrison, K and Ruch, G (2007) Social work and the use of self: on becoming a social worker, in Lymbery, M and Postle, K (eds) *Social work. A companion to learning.* London: Sage pp 40–50.

Hart, E and Bond, M (1995) *Action research for health and social care.* Buckingham: Open University Press.

Hawkins, P and Shohet, R (2007) *Supervising in the helping professions.* 3rd edn. Bucks: OUP.

Healy, K (2000) *Social work practices: contemporary perspectives on change.* London: Sage.

Healy, K and Mulholland, J. (2007) *Writing skills for social workers.* London: Sage.

Held, S (2009) Emotional intelligence, emotion and collaborative leadership, in McKimm, J and Philips, K (eds) *Leadership and management in integrated services.* Exeter: Learning Matters.

Henwood, S and Lister, J (2007) *NLP and Coaching for Health Care Professionals.* Chichester: Wiley.

HEPI (Higher Education Policy Institute) (2004) *Credit accumulation and transfer, and the Bologna process.* Bahram Bekhradnia: HEPI.

Higham, P (2006) Post qualifying social work education: flagships for social work or sinking ship? 8th UK Joint Social Work Education Conference. Crossing Boundaries: Personal, Professional, Political. Cambridge University, 12–14 July.

Holmes, T H and Rahe, R H (1967) The social re-adjustment rating scale. *Journal of Psychosomatic Research*, 11: 213–8.

Honey, P and Mumford, A (2008) Honey and Mumford learning styles questionnaire. Available from **www.peterhoney.com** (accessed 28 March 2009).

Howe, D (2008) *The emotionally intelligent social worker.* Basingstoke: Palgrave MacMillan.

Huczynski, A and Buchanan, D (2007) *Organisational behaviour.* 6th edn Harlow: Pearson.

Hudson, B (2002) Interprofessionality in health and social care: the Achilles heel of partnership. *Journal of Interprofessional Care*, 16(1): 7–17.

Hull, C, Redfern, and Shuttleworth, A (2004) *Profiles and portfolios: a guide for health and social care.* 2nd edn Basingstoke: Palgrave Macmillan.

Humphries, B (2008) *Social work research for social justice.* Basingstoke: Palgrave Macmillan.

Huxley, P, Evans, S, Gately, C, Webber, M, Mears, A, Pajak, S, Kendall, T, Medina, J and Katona, C (2005) Stress and pressures in mental health social work: the worker speaks. *British Journal of Social Work*, 35: 1063–79.

Ingleby, E (2006) *Applied psychology for social work.* Exeter: Learning Matters.

International Federation of Social Workers (2000) Definition of social work. Available from **www.ifsw.org/en/p38000208.html** (accessed 28 March 2009).

Jack, G (2004) *Ecological perspectives in assessing children and families,* in Horwath, J (2004) *The child's world: assessing children in need.* London: Jessica Kingsley Publishers, pp 53–74.

Jelphs, K and Dickinson, H (2008) *Working in teams.* Bristol: Policy Press.

Johns, C (1998) Opening the doors of perception, in Johns, C and Freshwater, D (eds) *Transforming nursing through reflective practice.* Oxford: Blackwell Science, pp 1–20.

Johnson, B (1996) *Polarity management: identifying and managing unsolvable problems.* 2nd ed. Amherst, MA: HRD Press.

Jones, C, Ferguson, I, Lavalette M, and Penketh, L (2004) *Social work and social justice: a manifesto for a new engaged practice.* Available from: **www.liv.ac.uk/sspsw/manifesto/manifesto.htm** (accessed 17 February 2009).

Jordan, B and Jordan, C (2006) *Social work and the third way: tough love as social policy.* 3rd edn, London: Sage.

Kamya, H (2000) Hardiness and spiritual well being among social work students: implications for social work education. *Journal of Social Work Education*, 36: 231–40.

Kadushin, A and Harkness, D (2002) *Supervision in social work.* 4th edn New York: Columbia University Press.

Keeping, C (2006) *Emotional aspects of the professional identity of social workers.* Bristol: University of the West of England/Avon and Wiltshire NHS.

Kneale, P (2003) Study skills for geography students. London: Hodder.

Kobasa (1969), in Kamya, H (2000) Hardiness and spiritual well being among social work students: implications for social work education. *Journal of Social Work Education*, 36: 231–40.

Koerin, B, Harrigan, M, and Reeves, J (1990) Facilitating the transition from student to social worker: challenges of the younger student. *Journal of Social Work Education*, 26: 199–208.

Laming, H (2003) *The Victoria Climbié Inquiry*, London: TSO. Available from **www.victoria-climbie-inquiry.org.uk** (accessed 2 February 2009).

Lawson, H (2004) The logic of collaboration in education and the human services. *Journal of Interprofessional Care*, 18(3): 225–37.

LLUK (Lifelong Learning UK) (2008) Pass on your skills initiative. Available from: **www.passonyourskills.com/about/about-poys.html**.

Lowes, L and Hulatt, I (eds) (2005) *Service users involvement in health and social care research.* London: Routledge.

Lymbery, M (2006) United we stand? Partnership working in health and social care and the role of social work in services for older people. *British Journal of Social Work*, 36: 1119–34.

Lyons, K and Manion, K (2004) Goodbye DipSW: trends in student satisfaction and employment outcomes. Some Implications for the New Social Work Award. *Social Work Education,* 23: 133–148.

McBride, P (1998) *The assertive social worker.* Aldershot: Ashgate.

McCloskey C (2006). *Evaluating the impact of post-qualifying social work programmes.* Bournemouth: Centre for Post-Qualifying Social Work, Bournemouth University.

McDonald, C (2007) This is who we are and this is what we do: social work education and self-efficacy. *Australian Social Work*, 60: 83–93.

Maddi, S, Kahn, S and Maddi, K (1998) The effectiveness of hardiness training. *Consulting Psychology Journal, Practice and Research*, 50: 78–86.

Maher, B, Appleton, C, Benge, D and Perham, T (2003) *The criticality of induction training to professional social work care and protection practice.* Paper presented to the ninth Australasian Conference on Child Abuse and Neglect: Sydney.

Marsh, P and Triseliotis, J (1996) *Ready to practice? Social workers and probation officers: their training and their first year in work.* Avebury: Aldershot.

Maunder, L and Cameron, L (2006) Stress: a self help guide. Northumberland Department of Psychological Services and Research, Newcastle, North Tyneside and Northumberland

Mental Health NHS Trust, St George's Hospital. Available from: **www.patient.co.uk/ showdoc/27001310/** (accessed 20 March 2009).

Mehra, A, Smith, B R, Dixon, A L and Robertson, B (2006) Distributed Leadership in Teams – the network of leadership perceptions and team performance. *The Leadership Quarterly*, 17: 232–45.

Miller, E and Cook, A (2007) *Users and cares define effective partnerships in health and social care. Modernising adult social care initiative*. Birmingham: University of Birmingham. Available from: **www.masc.bham.ac.uk/Reports/UCDEP.pdf** (accessed 23 February 2009).

Mitchell, C (2001) Partnership for continuing professional development: the impact of the Post Qualifying Award for Social Workers (PQSW) on social work practice. *Social Work Education*, 20: 433–45.

Moon, J (2005) *We seek it here . . . a new perspective on the elusive activity of critical thinking: a theoretical and practical approach*. Bristol: ESCalate.

Morhman, SA, Cohen, SG and Morhman, AM (1995) Designing team based organisations. San Francisco, CA: Jossey–Bass.

Moriarty, J and Murray, J. (2007) Who wants to be a social worker? *British Journal of Social Work*, 37: 715–33.

Morrison, T (2007) Emotional Intelligence, emotions and social work: Context, characteristics, complications and contribution. *British Journal of Social Work*, 37: 245–63.

Moscrip, S and Brown, A (2002) Child and youth care: The transition from student to practitioner. *The International Child and Youth Care Network*, 41. Available from: **www.cyc-net.org/cyc-online/cycol-0602-transitions.html** (accessed 14 July 2008).

MSC (Management Standards Centre) (2005) *The National Occupational Standards for Management and Leadership*. London: MSC.

MSH (Management Sciences for Health) and UNICEF (1998) *The Guide to Managing for Quality*. Available from: **http://erc.msh.org/quality/pstools/pspareto.cfm** (accessed 19 February 2009).

Newton, J N and McKenna, L (2006) The transitional journey through the graduate year: A focus group study. *International Journal of Nursing Studies*, 44: 1231–7.

Northern Ireland Government – Department for Health, Social Services and Public Safety. Record keeping, confidentiality and sharing information. Available from: **www.dhsspsni.gov.uk/safeguard_chpt8.pdf** (accessed 2 February 2009)

NISCC (2006) *Northern Ireland Post Qualifying Education and Training Framework in Social Work*. Belfast: NISCC.

NSWQB (2004) *Induction study – a study of the induction needs of newly qualified and non-nationally qualified social workers in health boards*. Dublin: NSWQB.

O'Connor, J (2006) *NLP workbook*. London: Thorsons.

OECD (Organisation for Economic Co-operation and Development) (2007) *Qualifications and Lifelong Learning. Policy Brief*. April 2007. Paris: OECD. Available from: **www.oecd.org/dataoecd/10/2/38500491.pdf** (accessed 20 August 2008).

Ogilvie-Whyte, S (2006) *Baselines: a review of evidence about the impact of education and training in childcare and protection on practice and client outcomes. Evaluation and evidence, discussion paper 2*. Dundee: Scottish Institute for Excellence in Social Work Education.

Pare, A and Le Maistre, C (2006) Active learning in the workplace: transforming individuals and institutions. *Journal of Education and Work*, 19: 363–81.

Parker, J (2004) *Effective practice learning in social work*, Exeter: Learning Matters.

Parker, J (2007) Developing effective practice learning for tomorrow's social workers, *Social Work Education*, 26: 763–79.

Parker, J and Bradley, G (2007) *Social work practice: assessment, planning, intervention and review*. 2nd edn Exeter: Learning Matters.

Parker, J, Whitfield, J and Doel, M (2006) *Effective practice learning in local authorities (2). Workforce development, recruitment and retention*. Leeds: Practice Learning Taskforce.

Parkes, C M (1971) Psychosocial transitions: a field study. *Social Science and Medicine*, 5: 101–115.

Paterson (2002), in Trevithick, P (2005) *Social work skills: a practice handbook*. 2nd edn Bucks: OUP.

Pawson, R, Boaz, A, Grayson, L, Long, A, and Barnes, C (2003) *Types and quality of knowledge in social care, SCIE Knowledge Review 7*. Bristol: Policy Press.

Payne, M (2000) Teamwork in multiprofessional care. Basingstoke: Macmillan.

Payne, M (2006) *What is professional social work*. 2nd ed, Basingstoke: Palgrave.

Penhale, B (2007) Ethics and charging for care, in Maclaren, S and Leathard, A *Ethics and Contemporary Challenges*, Bristol: Policy Press, pp 185–97.

Peters, T (1989) *The customer revolution* (video). BBC training videos. London: BBC.

Pietroni, P C (1991) Stereotypes or archetypes? A study of perceptions amongst health care students. *Journal of Social Work Practice*, 5: 61–9.

Phillipson, J (2002) Supervision and being supervised, in Adams, R, Dominelli, L and Payne, M (2002) *Critical practice in social work*. Basingstoke: Palgrave Macmillan, pp 244–51.

Postle, K, Edwards, C, Moon, R, Rumsey, H, Thomas, T (2002) Continuing professional development after qualification – partnerships, pitfalls and potential. *Social Work Education,* 21: 157–69.

Preston-Shoot, M (2000) Stumbling towards oblivion or discovering new horizons? Observations on the relationship between social work education and practice. *Journal of Social Work Practice,* 14 (2): 87–98.

Prince, K, Van De Wiel, M W J, Van der Vleuten, C P M, Boshuizen, H P A and Scherpbier, A J J A (2004) Junior doctors' opinions about the transition from medical school to clinical practice: a change of environment. *Education for Health*, 17: 323–31.

Quality Assurance Agency (2008) *Benchmarks for social work*. Available from **www.qaa.ac.uk/academicinfrastructure/benchmark/statements/socialwork08.pdf** (accessed 28 March 2009).

Quinney, A (2006) *Collaborative social work practice.* Exeter: Learning Matters.

Quinney, A, Thomas, J and Whittington, C (2009) *Working together to assess needs, strengths and risks.* London: SCIE.

Revans, L (2008) Keeping a head above water: NQSW. *Community Care,* 81: 14–15.

Rolfe, G, Freshwater D and Jasper, M (2001) *Critical thinking for nursing and the helping professions.* Hants: Palgrave.

Ronka, A, Oravala, S and Pulkkinen, L (2003) Time points in adults' lives: the effect of gender and amount of choice. *Journal of Adult Development* 10(3): 203–15.

Rose, W (2004) Assessing children in need and their families. An overview of the framework, in Horwath, J (2004) *The child's world. Assessing children in Need.* London: Jessica Kingsley Publishers, pp 35–49

Ross, I (2004) *NLP in business – modelling conflict resolution. ReSource.* London: Porto Publishing.

Rossi, P H, Lispey, M W and Freeman, H E (2004) *Evaluation: A systematic approach.* 7th edn Thousand Oaks, CA: Sage.

Ruch, G (2005) Relationship-based practice: holistic approaches to contemporary childcare social work. *Child and Family Social Work,* 10: 111–23.

Rubin, A, Johnson, P J and De Weaver, K L (1986) Direct practice interests of MSW students: changes from entry to graduation. *Journal of Social Work Education,* 22: 98–108.

Rushton, A and Martyn, H (1990) Two post-qualifying courses in social work: the views of the course members and their employees. *British Journal of Social Work,* 20: 445–68.

Sale, A U (2007) Easing into the job. *Community Care,* 1674: 42–4.

Sarason, SB and Lorentz, EM (1998) Crossing boundaries: collaboration, co-ordination and the redefinition of resources. San Francisco, CA: Jossey–Bass.

Schrader, A (2008) Hitchhiking across cultures from the classroom to the workplace. *Feliciter,* 2: 43–4.

SCIE (Social Care Institute for Excellence) (2006a) Knowledge about learning organisations. Available from: **www.scie.org.uk/publications/learningorgs/know/index.asp** (accessed 23 January 2009).

SCIE (2006b) *Learning Organisation Audit.* Available from **www.scie.org.uk/publications/learningorgs/files/key_characteristics_2.pdf** (accessed 10 February 2009).

SCIE (2007) *People Management Website.* Available on: **www.scie-peoplemanagement.org.uk** (accessed 1 May 2007).

Seden, J (2007) *Assessing the needs of children and their families. Research and practice briefings: children and families, 15.* Totnes: Research and Practice. Available from: **www.rip.org.uk/publications/researchbriefings.asp** (accessed 26 March 2009).

Sellick, K (2008) Children's social workers give degree poor marks. *Community Care.* 29 May 2008: 5.

Senge, P M (1990) *The fifth discipline. The art and practice of the learning organisation.* London: Random House.

Seymour, C and Seymour, R (2007) *Courtroom skills for social workers.* Exeter: Learning Matters.

Sinclair, I (2008) Inspection: A quality-control perspective, in Davies, M (ed) *The Blackwell companion to social work.* 3rd edn Oxford: Blackwell, pp 449–57.

Skills for Care (2006) *Continuing professional development strategy for the social care workforce,* Leeds: Skills for Care.

Skills for Care/Children's Workforce Development Council (2007) *Providing Effective Supervision.* Leeds: SfC/CWDC. Available from **www.skillsforcare.org.uk/developing_ skills/leadership_and_management/providing_effective_supervision.aspx?** or **www. cwdcouncil.org.uk/assets/0000/2832/providing_effective_supervision_unit.pdf** (accessed 17 February 2009).

Skills for Care (2008) *Newly qualified social workers.* Leeds: Skills for Care. Available from: **www.skillsforcare.org.uk/developing_skills/social_work/newlyqualifiedsocialworkers. aspx?** (accessed 29 January 2009).

Skinner, K (2005) *Continuing professional development for the social services workforce in Scotland.* Developing learning organisations, discussion paper 1. Dundee: Scottish Institute for Excellence in Social Work Education.

SSSC (Scottish Social Services Council) (2005) *Rules and requirements for specialist training for social services workers in Scotland.* Dundee: SSSC.

Stanley, N, Manthorpe, J and White, M (2007) Depression in the profession: social workers' experiences and perceptions. *British Journal of Social Work,* 37: 281–98.

Stapleton, S R (1998) Team building: making collaborative practice work. *Journal of Nurse-Midwifery,* 43: 12–18.

Storey, J and Billingham, J (2001) Occupational stress and social work. *Social Work Education,* 20: 659–70.

Swinton, L (2008) *Honey and Mumford – learning style questionnaire.* Available from: **www.mftrou.com/honey-mumford.html** (accessed 26 August 2008).

Taylor, C (1999) Experiences of a pilot project for the post qualifying award in social work. *Social Work Education,* 18: 71–82.

Thomas, J, Whittington, C and Quinney, A (2009a) *Building relationships, establishing trust and negotiating with other workers.* London: SCIE.

Thomas, J, Whittington, C and Quinney, A (2009b) *Working collaboratively in different types of teams.* London: SCIE.

Tickle, L (2007) The heat is on. *Community Care.* 15 November 2007, pp 37–39. Available from: **www.communitycare.co.uk/articles/2007/11/15/106467/burnout-in-the-work-place-a-case-of-too-much-too-soon-for-young-social-workers.html** (accessed 31 March 2009).

Townsley, R, Abbott, D and Watson D (2004) *Making a difference? Exploring the impact of multi-agency working on disabled children with complex health care needs, their families and the professionals who support them.* Bristol: Policy Press.

Topss England (2000) *Modernising the social care workforce.* Leeds: Topss England.

Topss England (2002) *National Occupational Standards for Social Care.* Leeds: Topss England. Now available from: **www.skillsforcare.org.uk/developing_skills/social_work/nos_for_social_work.aspx?** (accessed 16 February 2009).

Topss England (2004) (now *Skills for Care) Workforce Planning Toolkit.* Leeds: Topss England.

Trevithick, P (2005) *Social work skills: a practice handbook.* 2nd edn Bucks: OUP.

Tsui, M (2005) *Social work supervision: contexts and concepts.* London: Sage.

Tuckman, B (1965) Developmental sequence in small groups. *Psychological Bulletin,* 63(6): 384–99.

Turner, M, Brough, P and Williams-Findlay, R B (2003) *Our voice in our future: service users debate the future of the welfare state.* London: Shaping our Lives National User Network.

Unrau, Y A, Gabor, P A and Grinnell, R M (2007) *Evaluation in social work: the art and science of practice.* 4th edn, New York: Oxford University Press.

Walker, J, Crawford, K and Parker, J (2008) *Practice education in social work: a handbook for practice teachers, assessors and educators.* Exeter: Learning Matters.

Walker, S, Shemmings, D and Cleaver, H (2005) *Write Enough: interactive training materials to support quality recording in children's social services,* **www.writeenough.org.uk** (accessed 2 February 2009).

Walter, I, Nutley, S, Percy-Smith, J, McNeish, D, and Frost, S (2004) *Improving the use of research in social care practice (Knowledge review 7).* London: SCIE and The Policy Press.

Wangensteen, S, Johansson, I S, Nordstrom, G (2008) The first year as a graduate nurse – an experience of growth and development. *Journal of Clinical Nursing,* 17: 1877–85

Warren, J (2007) *Service users and carer participation in social work.* Exeter: Learning Matters.

Watson, T J (2002) *Organising and managing work. Organisational, managerial and strategic behaviour in theory and practice.* Harlow: Pearson Education.

Weick, K (1995) *Sensemaking in organizations.* Thousand Oaks, CA: Sage Publications.

Wenger, E (1998) *Communities of practice: learning, meaning and identity.* Cambridge: Cambridge University Press.

Wenger, E C (2006). *Communities of practice: a brief introduction.* Available from: **www.ewenger.com/theory/index.htm** (accessed 23 January 2009).

Whittington, C (2003). A model of collaboration, in Weinstein J, Whittington, C and Leiba T (eds) *Collaboration in social work practice.* London: Jessica Kingsley, pp 39–62.

Whittington, C (2007) *SCIE Guide 18: assessment in social work: a guide for learning and teaching.* London: SCIE. Available from: **www.scie.org.uk/publications/resourceguides/rg08/teaching/index.asp** (accessed 29 January 2009).

Whittington, C, Thomas J and Quinney A (2009a) *An introduction to interprofessional and interagency collaboration.* London: SCIE.

Whittington, C, Thomas, J and Quinney, A (2009b) *Professional identity and collaboration.* London: SCIE.

Woodward, C and Potanin, F (2004) *Winning: the story of England's rise to world cup glory.* London: Hodder and Stoughton.

Index